INTERNATIONAL ASPECTS OF ORGANIZATIONAL ETHICS IN EDUCATIONAL SYSTEMS

STUDIES IN EDUCATIONAL ADMINISTRATION

Series Editors: Gaëtane Jean-Marie and Ann E. Lopez

Studies in Educational Administration presents monographs and edited collections along the broad themes of educational leadership, management and administration.

The series presents research conducted across a diverse range of contexts and locations. Proposals are invited for authored or edited books from scholars in all stages of their careers for work that will help us to advance the educational administration field, and will be of use to both researchers and school administrators and teachers.

Forthcoming Publications

Alison Taysum and Khalid Arar (eds), *Turbulence, Empowerment and Marginalized Groups in International Education Governance Systems*

Izhar Oplatka and Khalid Arar (eds), *Emotion Management in Teaching and Educational Leadership: A Cultural Perspective*

Interested in publishing in this series? Please contact Gaëtane Jean-Marie and Ann E. Lopez at sea@uni.edu

INTERNATIONAL ASPECTS OF ORGANIZATIONAL ETHICS IN EDUCATIONAL SYSTEMS

BY

ORLY SHAPIRA-LISHCHINSKY
Bar-llan University, Israel

United Kingdom – North America – Japan – India – Malaysia – China

Emerald Publishing Limited
Howard House, Wagon Lane, Bingley BD16 1WA, UK

First edition 2018

Copyright © 2018 Emerald Publishing Limited

Reprints and permissions service
Contact: permissions@emeraldinsight.com

British Library Cataloguing in Publication Data
A catalogue record for this book is available from the British Library

ISBN: 978-1-78714-778-2 (Print)
ISBN: 978-1-78714-777-5 (Online)
ISBN: 978-1-78743-018-1 (Epub)

Printed and bound by CPI Group (UK) Ltd, Croydon, CR0 4YY

ISOQAR certified
Management System,
awarded to Emerald
for adherence to
Environmental
standard
ISO 14001:2004.

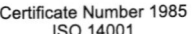

Certificate Number 1985
ISO 14001

INVESTOR IN PEOPLE

In Memory of Professor Paul T. Begley, My Authentic Leader

Sponsored by

MARIE SKŁODOWSKA-CURIE – Individual Fellowships, Horizon 2020
European Commission

The Schintzer Foundation for Research on the Israeli Economy and Society,
Bar-Ilan University

The Vice President for Research of Bar-Ilan University

Acknowledgments

I would like to thank my colleagues: researchers, school principals, supervisors, school counselors, teachers, educational administrators, human resource managers in different educational systems, and directors in the educational systems of local municipalities. Their curiosity about the research on organizational ethics, their drive to understand how ethical codes for educators and teachers have been developed and integrated across nations, and their real desire to reduce teachers' withdrawal behaviors encouraged me to write this book. I wish to thank all of my mentees, who were studying for their Masters' degrees and doctorates, for the learning process that we experienced together undertaken by working closely in educational field. I also thank the educational leaders, responsible for human resources, in educational systems throughout the world, who had a real desire to offer solutions for reduction of teachers' withdrawal behaviors.

Further thanks go to the Marie Sklodowska-Curie Individual Fellowships, Horizon 2020, European Commission; Schintzer Foundation for Research on the Israeli Economy and Society, Bar-Ilan University; and the Vice President for Research of Bar-Ilan University for support and help in sponsoring this book. I would like to thank Suzanna Levin for her designing of the figures, and Dr. Julia Chaitin for her help in reviewing this book. Finally, I would like to thank my mother, Dalya, and my core family, Alon, Yaarit, Aaron, Arad, and Yogev, for their emotional and cognitive support throughout this project. I love you!

Contents

List of Figures

List of Tables

List of Cases

List of Questionnaires

About the Author

Orly Shapira-Lishchinsky is an Associate Professor in the largest Israeli Department of Administration and Leadership in Educational Systems in the School of Education at Bar-Ilan University. She is also a Member of the Ethics Board of the university. Professor Shapira-Lishchinsky was a Visiting Scholar and Instructor at Fordham University, the University of Missouri-Columbia, and the University of Alabama, and she was a Research Scholar at the State University of New York, in Albany, NewYork.

She began her career in the educational system as a high school Chemistry teacher and homeroom teacher, and continued as a Mentor for science and technology teachers. Professor Shapira-Lishchinksy headed a project for the integration of science and technology in the Ort educational network in Israel.

Professor Shapira-Lishchinksy's research focuses on the relationships between perceptions of organizational ethics and teachers' withdrawal behaviors, such as tardiness, absences, and the tendency to leave. Her work explores the development of ethical codes in educational systems throughout the world through strategies of leadership and expertise and facilitation of group simulations. Her recent studies compare different educational systems of the world.

Professor Shapira-Lishchinksy's research has been published in leading academic journals that focus on educational administration, including: *Educational Administration Quarterly, Journal of Educational Administration,* and *Educational Management Administration & Leadership.* She has lectured at prestigious conferences, such as the AERA, CIES, ECER, and the UCEA. In addition, Professor Shapira-Lishchinksy is on the editorial board of the *International Journal of Educational Management* and the *Journal of Education and Training Studies.* Her research has been funded by different foundations, including the Marie Sklodowska-Curie, the Shalem Foundation, and the Israeli Ministry of Education. Professor Shapira-Lishchinksy also serves as an Expert of Research Services for the head scientist at the Israeli Ministry of Education.

Foreword

This book was written because of the real need to dispel some of the ambiguity and uncertainty found in the international research and in the educational field concerning the meanings of the concept "organizational ethics" among educational leaders and teachers. This ambiguity is found across nations and is a characteristic of different educational systems. It produces uncertainty concerning different responses of educational leaders and teachers to ethical cases. This uncertainty can lead to a decrease in the status of educational leaders and teachers, since teachers may express insecurity concerning how they should behave when faced with an ethical issue.

The multitude of inappropriate behaviors among educational leaders and teachers harms the teaching profession, the quality of teaching, the schools's learning processes, and its scholastic achievements. Therefore, in order to lower the ambiguity surrounding these ethical cases, to empower the teaching profession, and to improve the educational systems' effectiveness, many countries throughout the world have developed ethical codes that are designed for educational leaders and teachers.

The goal of this book is to focus on organizational ethical aspects in the international context in different educational systems of the world, through the development of an integrative approach. It centers on teachers' withdrawal behaviors and the development of an ethical code for educators and teachers, which can serve as a tool for reducing misbehaviors and withdrawal behaviors among teachers. By discussing the leading ethical predictors for withdrawal behaviors, and considering personal and organizational characteristics, this book can contribute to an understanding of the perceptions and attitudes which that lead to teachers' tardiness, absenteeism, turnover, and attrition in educational systems.

In light of this, the book is divided into four main sections.

The first section focuses on the expression of ethics in the international context by relating to both national culture and global culture. As part of understanding the international aspects of the concept of ethics, by considering educational systems, this section discusses the characteristics of teachers' behaviors in ethical schools. Such a process can lead to the emergence of the concept of ethical school culture – a concept that has not yet been investigated in educational systems via an organizational perspective. In this section, I present an integrative approach, simultaneously considering the concept of ethical school culture, in addition to traditional factors, such as internal and external school factors, in order to explain inequalities in students' achievements.

This section also deals with the development and the assimilation of an ethical code in a number of different countries as a tool for dealing with ethical challenges in varied educational systems. The development of an ethical code for educators and teachers, and its assimilation in different educational systems of the world, can help lower the ambiguity surrounding ways to deal with ethical events that faced by educational leaders and teachers face. As a result, it can help empower the teaching profession, promote teacher education for social justice, and help advance quality educational systems across nations.

The second section focuses on the international aspects of ethics in the context of school leadership. This section discusses training processes and focuses mainly on the moral dimension of leadership – authentic leadership of school principals – while describing additional leadership styles imbued with ethical meanings, such as transactional and transformational leadership styles. It focuses on ethical dilemmas faced by educational leaders and provides help for the decision-making process that concerns ethical decisions.

The third section focuses on ethical perceptions of teachers, personal and organizational characteristics, and organizational commitment that predict teachers' withdrawal behaviors such as tardiness, absenteeism, turnover, and attrition.

In this section, the teachers' withdrawal behaviors serve as the criteria for the ethical challenges that concern all people working in educational systems across nations – from the level of teachers, educational coordinators, principals, supervisors, and district administrations of the ministries of education. While most of the studies on withdrawal behaviors of teachers have focused on socioeconomic factors in order to explain teachers' withdrawal behaviors, such as gender, seniority, and age, this book raises ethical aspects from the field that have not yet been studied in relation to withdrawal behaviors.

I also describe the concept of organizational citizenship behavior, which is generally perceived as the opposite behavior of withdrawal behaviors, in this section. In addition, I discuss the characteristics of the relationship between teachers' organizational citizenship behaviors and teachers' withdrawal behaviors. At the end of this section, I present updated studies that have explored the relationship between ethical perceptions and withdrawal behaviors and organizational citizenship behaviors, including strategies and learner-centered education, for minimizing withdrawal behaviors in educational systems.

The fourth section of the book focuses on the applications of the topics previously presented and discussed previously. It explores how educational leaders throughout the world can deal with ethical challenges in educational systems by employing analyses of critical ethical incidents in group simulations. Furthermore, the section presents the gap between official policy and practice and innovative research in the area as well as the scenarios to use in different training frameworks.

The book's content can lead to plans of action for educational leaders across nations – those working in the headquarters of the ministries of education, in the schools, and in the educational departments of local municipalities. These plans of action can help minimize withdrawal behaviors and promote organizational citizenship behavior among teachers, and can help the schools increase excellent achievements and minimization of social gaps.

The discussion about the development of the ethical code, from an international viewpoint, which also demonstrates how the processes work in different countries, can influence functionaries and educational leaders, in different strata, who are in charge of human resources in educational systems. It can help educational leaders and teachers, across nations, to formulate ideas for developing, updating, and assimilating an ethical educational code by designing and facilitating educational programs and workshops. This ethical code can also help facilitate the definition of roles of teachers, help empower them, minimize inappropriate behaviors, and increase school effectiveness.

The book allows for the development of an integrative approach for coping with ethical challenges among educational leaders and teachers and connects theory to praxis. In light of the fact that many people throughout the world deal, in one way or another, with ethical challenges, this book is relevant for researchers and students in the field of administration and leadership in educational systems. It is also relevant for stakeholders interested in human resources in educational organizations at headquarters' level, in administrative and supervisory positions, directors in departments of education at the local level, and functionaries in school leadership, such as principals, vice principals, and pedagogical coordinators.

In sum, I believe that the strength of this book is derived from the fact that it developed from the fieldwork. I was a chemistry teacher and a homeroom teacher in a high school, as well as a mentor and a project manager for science education. Today, I am in research and teach in the academic world. As a result, the book presents an academic perception while also connecting to the field.

Section I

International Aspects of Ethics

Chapter 1

The Ethical Context: A Global Versus a National Approach

The concept of ethics focuses on perceptions, attitudes, and behaviors that include valuating, choosing, and acting, and taking into consideration desirable actions that connect to the notions of human rights and having responsibility for others (Rausch, Lindquist, & Steckel, 2014; Smith & Smith, 2016). There are two main approaches to ethics and culture. The first one emphasizes *differences* in moral perceptions and moral judgments among cultures (Melé & Sánchez-Runde, 2013). Researchers, who adopt this approach, perceive ethical national culture as influencing ethical perceptions and behaviors in organizations (Minkov & Hofstede, 2011).

House, Hanges, Javidan, Dorfman, and Gupta (2004), in their Global Leadership and Organizational Behavior Effectiveness (GLOBE) project, defined national culture as the common experience of individuals. This common experience results in the members of the culture developing shared values, beliefs, policies, and interpretations of meaningful events. As a result, members tend to perceive the world in distinctive ways. Minkov and Hofstede (2011) created a four-dimensional (4D) model of national culture that adopts this perspective, has become a cornerstone for cross-cultural research, and reflects current social values and practices (Shiraev & Levy, 2015).

For example, research based on the first approach has found that cultural differences influence individuals' ethical reasoning skills (Christians, Fackler, Richardson, Kreshel, & Woods, 2015). Furthermore, Forsyth, O'Boyle, and McDaniel (2008) undertook a meta-analysis of research from 29 different countries and found Western countries exhibit a more pragmatist ethic, while Eastern and Middle Eastern countries were found to be more subjective concerning moral rules. In another study, Ho (2010) uncovered differences in the ethical perceptions of Malay, Chinese, and Indian leaders. He found that cultural differences focus on various ethical attributes of moral dilemma. Li and Persons (2010), who undertook a comparative study between Chinese and American students, which used an experimental corporate code of ethics, found that cultural differences resulted in less ethical decision making in the former group than in the latter group.

International Aspects of Organizational Ethics in Educational Systems, 3–4
Copyright © 2018 by Emerald Publishing Limited
All rights of reproduction in any form reserved
doi:10.1108/978-1-78714-777-520181001

In comparison to the first approach, which emphasizes cultural distinctiveness, the second approach avers that we need to acknowledge the existence of a *global* ethical culture vis-à-vis perception of ethics. An example of research based on this school of thought comes from the work of Cullen, Parboteeah, and Hoegl (2004). These scholars used the institutional anomie theory to develop hypotheses related to four national culture variables (achievement, individualism, universalism, and pecuniary materialism) and found cross-national consistency of perceptions regarding ethically suspect behaviors. Other researchers, who have supported the existence of a universal minimal morality, have demonstrated that collective survival necessitates the universal adoption of certain basic values (Donnelly, 2013; Ivison, 2010).

Empirical studies have also shown that, beyond moral judgment in specific cases, there are core values or principles which are at the basis of these judgments and appear in the major world religions and traditions (Bok, 2002; Terry, 2011, Tullberg, 2015). As noted by Melé and Sánchez-Runde (2013), it also appears that a global approach is essential for supporting and facilitating the application of a universal ethical policy in human rights that has been detailed in important documents pertaining to human rights. Examples of these documents include the Universal Declaration of Human Rights and other UN human rights covenants, texts, and principles, such as the UN Global Compact and its 10 ethical principles.

In the field of education, research has been undertaken on *national ethical culture*, which adopts the approach of cultural diversity and dissimilarity among different countries. These studies have explored ethical issues, such as social justice (Banks, 2015), ethical dilemmas (Milner & Tenore, 2010), and developing student potential (Klassen, Usher, & Bong, 2010). On the other hand, different studies have focused on the existence of a *global ethical culture*, which is based on notions of universalism and similarity. Studies have examined topics, such as human rights in educational systems (Stromquist & Monkman, 2014), reducing gaps (Zhao, 2010), and quality education (Wang, 2011). For example, one of the goals of international assessment, such as Trends in International Mathematics and Science Study (TIMSS) and Programme for International Student Assessment, is to promote equity policies that can help narrow achievement gaps and reduce differences in text scores between higher and lower scoring groups (Mullis, Martin, Foy, & Hooper, 2016). In order to achieve this goal, participating countries design educational policies that take into consideration shared ethical values, such as promoting the potential development of students by maximizing the performance of students who have generally been low achievers (Hanushek & Woessmann, 2015).

The most up-to-date research based on TIMSS 2015 questionnaires (Shapira-Lishchinsky, 2018a) reveals that in order to better understand organizational ethics, we should consider the combination of universal values and national values. In other words, we should explore the global values that are common in different countries while understanding that their effects may differ in the countries, and these differences will be reflected by different student academic achievements.

Chapter 2

The Code of Ethics in Educational Systems: International Aspects

In order to explore similarities or differences between global and national ethical values, it is worthwhile to compare the codes of ethics for teachers and educators that are developed in different countries. In the following chapters, I will define the meaning of codes of ethics in educational systems while comparing general values and categories in randomly selected countries.

A code of ethics is a document created by a professional association, occupational regulatory body, or another professional body that aims to provide guidance for the practitioners who are its members, to protect service users, and to safeguard the profession's reputation (Bullough, 2011; Van Nuland, 2011). In order to construct the codes of ethics, the authoritative body writing the code seeks advice from experts and undertakes a thorough consultation process with internal and external stakeholders (Shapiro & Gross, 2013; Singh, 2006).

There is wide agreement that codes of ethics cover the most important and relevant ethical norms applicable to organizations (Carasco & Singh, 2003; Shapiro & Stefkovich, 2016). In order to adhere to the code of ethics, organizations install checks to ensure that their code includes relevant ethical norms, or, at the very least, does not support norms that conflict with interests and views held by the organization's stakeholders and the community at large.

In educational systems, the main goal of a code of ethics is to provide self-disciplinary guidelines through the formulation of necessary ethical norms and standards of professional conduct (Maxwell & Schwimmer, 2016). When a code of ethics determines the boundaries for what is considered accepted behavior, this can help educational leaders solve conflicts of interest in a balanced and flexible manner (Shapiro & Stefkovich, 2010). The codes can specifically provide guidance for professional ethics, concretely support these ethics, protect the well-being of students, and work to minimize misconduct of teachers and principals toward one another. Finally, it can be instrumental in promoting public trust in schools (Poisson, 2009).

In most countries, codes of ethics in educational systems are developed and periodically updated on the basis of organizational perspectives held by stakeholders in the educational system. These parties include representatives from the government and teachers' unions, school principals, and supervisors (Maxwell &

International Aspects of Organizational Ethics in Educational Systems, 5–12
Copyright © 2018 by Emerald Publishing Limited
All rights of reproduction in any form reserved
doi:10.1108/978-1-78714-777-520181002

Schwimmer, 2016). As a result, a code of ethics for teachers and educators may uncover ethical aspects of everyday school practices that connect to ethical policy, ethical norms and standards of professional conduct, expected shared values, and desirable ethical behavior for teachers.

When examining codes of ethics for educators and teachers from 30 different countries in the world, it was found that these codes relate to the following five main categories that reflect global values (Shapira-Lishchinsky, 2018b):

1. The ethical aspect of caring for the students (e.g., the student's well-being, respect of the student's culture, the student's safety, meeting the needs of the student, and the student's knowledge and skills).
2. The ethical aspect of the teachers' profession (e.g., professional development, evaluation and supervision, quality of the teaching, and serving as a role model).
3. The ethical aspect of relations with colleagues (e.g., respecting peers, maintaining secrecy, cooperation, emotional support, and not causing harm).
4. The ethical aspect concerning parents and the community (e.g., parental involvement, respecting the parents' culture, and safeguarding discreetness and connections between school activities and the community).
5. The ethical aspect of respecting the law, school regulations, and students' rights (e.g., respecting the democratic system, and respecting the system of law and government policies).

The first category, "caring for the students," reflects the idea that such caring should mainly focus on caring for the well-being of the students, rather than caring for their learning potential. Specifically, this category highlights important ethical aspects, such as fairness, equality, respecting other cultures, and maintaining confidentiality. The analysis of the codes from the 30 nations revealed that stakeholders in education, who develop teachers' code of ethics in each country, still assume that it is important to focus on developing student potential by engaging in formal learning and in informal strategies to help their students develop creative thinking.

The second category, "teachers' profession," reflects that stakeholders in educational systems expect teachers to promote ethics in educational systems through a number of ways. They need to adhere to high standards, be accountable in the educational process, demonstrate their commitment to ongoing professional learning, and promote and maintain the status of teachers by protecting the reputation of the profession and by providing a role model within the educational institutions as well as in the community and in other social spheres.

The third category, "relations with colleagues," focuses on teachers' initiatives that promote collaborative learning between colleagues. Such initiatives can foster support between colleagues as they attempt to successfully deal with ethical aspects, such as inequality among students. This category also includes ethical aspects of "caring for colleagues," and can be expressed, for example, in doing one's best to treat colleagues in a just and equitable way, engaging in positive cooperation, in which all opinions are treated with respect, and honoring the privacy of their colleagues.

"Parents' and community's involvement" is the fourth ethical category. This reflects caring for the student by informing parents about their children's academic status as well as their well-being. It also includes the importance of respecting parental responsibility and confidentiality. Epstein, Galindo, and Sheldon (2011) and Lawson (2003) showed that teachers are often unenthusiastic about asking parents to become involved in the school. While they understand the significant role that parents play in the development and empowerment of their children, in practice, they are wary of parental intervention. Results from these studies may shed light on the emphasis reflected in this category concerning the encouragement of teachers to seek actively parental involvement. The aim of this ethical category is to minimize the gap between teachers' understandings concerning the importance of parental involvement and their concrete attempts to involve parents in the school lives of their children.

The second facet of this category connects to community involvement, such as the school's contribution to the community. This can be accomplished by promoting a democratic community and preparing students to work in the community. This category also emphasizes how the community can contribute to the school. Examples of this include working with the community to support school programs that promote equal opportunities for all students, offering professional help in school decision making and actions, helping schools uphold their reputations, and building community trust and confidence in the educational system.

In any case, inclusion of the ethical aspect of parental and community involvement in codes reflects the understanding that ethical schools cannot be closed educational systems but rather must be open educational systems so that knowledge and information can flow between the school and the community. By engaging in this mutual exchange, the educational system can advance goals that promote equity and opportunity for all students.

The fifth grouping focuses on "respecting the law, school regulations, and students' rights." This category addresses ethical aspects that include the importance of abiding by the rules, since these rules are designed to protect human rights of all the students and the teachers connected with the schools. The category aims to create a balance between the independence of the teacher and school regulations and guidelines in cases that teachers perceive a conflict or a tension between their understandings and the school's rules.

Educational systems encourage teachers to follow the rules of their institutions as long as these rules do not pressure the teacher into engaging in activities that conflict with his/her professional ethics. When conflicts arise, it is expected that teachers will search for ways to uphold the regulations while continuing to act according to their personal values and ethics.

Table 2.1 presents a detailed presentation of the dimensions that emerged from the analysis of codes of ethics in educational systems from three randomly selected countries – Slovenia, the United States, and Thailand. The analysis of these codes of ethics demonstrates that there are global ethical values reflecting a universal ethical culture, such as: caring for students, teachers' profession, relationships between teachers and their colleagues, parental and community involvement, and respecting the rules. However, the findings also demonstrate

Table 2.1: Analyzing Codes of Ethics in Educational Systems: Slovenia, the United States, and Thailand.

Country	Code Title	Caring for Students	Teachers' Profession	Relationships between Teachers and Their Colleagues	Parental and Community Involvement	Respecting the Rules
Slovenia	Code of ethics for members of the National Association of Catholic Pedagogues	• Provision of equal opportunities for students • Respecting uniqueness of each student • Acceptance of the student in a holistic sense, including performance that needs improvement • Prevention of violent, disruptive, and harmful influences on students • Accepting the student's need to be treated as if s/he were at home	Ensuring teachers' reputations by stressing professional and responsible work	Increasing quality work and promoting professional growth through ongoing interaction with colleagues (either individually or through group work)	*Parents:* • Cooperating with parents on important missions related to their children's education • Making sure that parents are familiar with the school's values, goals, and resources • Dealing discretely with information about the families of students *Community:* Cooperating with institutions outside school in order to promote educational process	• Respecting school authorities • Behaving according to school and State laws/regulations

Country	Code Title	Caring for Students	Teachers' Profession	Relationships between Teachers and Their Colleagues	Parental and Community Involvement	Respecting the Rules
USA	The Association of American Educators (AAE) code of ethics for educators	• Maintaining confidentiality of students' information, unless report is required by law • Protecting students from conditions that harm learning, health, or safety	• Responsibility and accountability for teachers' performance • Participating in professional growth	• Maintaining confidentiality of colleagues' information unless report is required by law • Respecting one's colleagues	*Community:* • Cooperation between the school and community is essential due to awareness that quality education is the common goal of the public, Boards of Education, and educators • Teachers play an active role in encouraging relationships between the school and the community *Parents* • Real efforts are made for an open communication with parents in order to promote student development • There is respect for the values and traditions of the students' diverse cultures	Problems are solved, and discipline is also used, according to law and school policy School resources are used only for the promotion of school needs and not for personal reasons

Table 2.1: (*Continued*)

Country	Code Title	Caring for Students	Teachers' Profession	Relationships between Teachers and Their Colleagues	Parental and Community Involvement	Respecting the Rules
Thailand	Regulation of the Teachers' Council of Thailand on professional standards and ethics (2005)	• Encouraging students on an equal basis • Promoting development of students on physical, intellectual, mental, emotional, and social aspects	• Maintaining professional standards of experience • Completing practical training in educational institutions • Passing criteria for evaluation of practical training determined by the Teachers Council of Thailand Board • Improvement of practice, personality, and vision to maintain academic and social development	Provision of mutual support and promotion of synergy among educators	Constructive cooperation with one another in the community	Adherence to the democratic regime and with the King – the head of state

that each nation may differently interpret these dimensions, focusing on different aspects of these dimensions, based on their specific culture, norms, and educational experiences.

Fig. 2.1 presents an overview of the main categories and the subcategories of each category. For example, the first category, caring for the student, includes the subcategories: student well-being and developing students' potential. The second category, teachers' profession, includes the subcategories: quality of education and teachers' status. The third category, collegial relationships, includes the subcategories: caring for colleagues and collaborative learning. The fourth category, respecting the law and regulations, includes the subcategories: balancing between autonomy and regulation, and following the rules. Finally, the category parental and community involvement includes the subcategories: informing parents and respecting parents.

Taken together, these categories may generate the meaning of an "ethical school culture" and these highlight many important interactions taking place between the school stakeholders – the students, teachers, parents, and community – in order to promote ethical culture in school.

Awareness of these dimensions can promote teachers' understanding concerning the expectation of their roles, which may reveal ethical responses and

Fig. 2.1: The Multidimensional Model of Ethical School Culture
(© Susannah Levin, 2018).

behaviors toward their school principals, colleagues, students, parents, and community. In addition, this multidimensional model of "ethical school culture" may help educational leaders, who develop codes of ethics, whether on the school or national levels, use these dimensions and codes as a basis for brainstorming, for arriving at ideas for improvement, for learning from mistakes in codes developed for educators and teachers that were developed in the past, and for the design of the best code of ethics for them.

Chapter 3

An Integrative Model of Student Inequality: Ethical School Culture, and External and Internal School Factors

In this chapter, I will present an integrative model, emphasizing the importance of ethical school culture, in addition to external and internal school factors in promoting equality among students. This suggested model may be relevant for a variety of educational systems in the world.

In the area of academic achievement, beginning with Coleman's classic study and its early critiques (Coleman et al., 1966; Smith 1972) and in a multitude of subsequent studies (e.g., Gamoran, Secada, & Marrett, 2000), conventional models in the sociology of education tested hypotheses regarding the influence of a school's organizational attributes – for example, size (e.g., number of students), resources (e.g., expenditure per student), and professional development – on student achievements (e.g., Benito, Alegre & Gonzàlez-Balletbò, 2014). Initially, these models attempted to explain substantial inequalities in educational opportunity by drawing sharp distinctions between internal school constructs (such as the aforementioned ones) and external constructs, such as those located beyond the school (such as home background, socioeconomic status, and family structure).

Many subsequent lines of inquiry that focused on the overriding impact of either internal school factors or external home background factors on student performance continued to reinforce the conceptual divide between internal and external constructs (Bouhlila, 2015). For example, many empirical studies claimed that student performance fundamentally depends on school-based processes, such as establishing a positive and safe learning environment (e.g., Brault, Janosz, & Archambault, 2014). However, this literature rarely presents or discusses analytical constructs transcending, bridging, or linking internal factors with external ones.

While suggesting an integrative approach, I do not seek to determine whether, and under what conditions, school attributes or home background factors are more critical predictors of variation in student achievement. Recent research suggests that both sets of factors are important to different degrees (e.g., Yoshino, 2012).

International Aspects of Organizational Ethics in Educational Systems, 13–16
Copyright © 2018 by Emerald Publishing Limited
doi:10.1108/978-1-78714-777-520181003

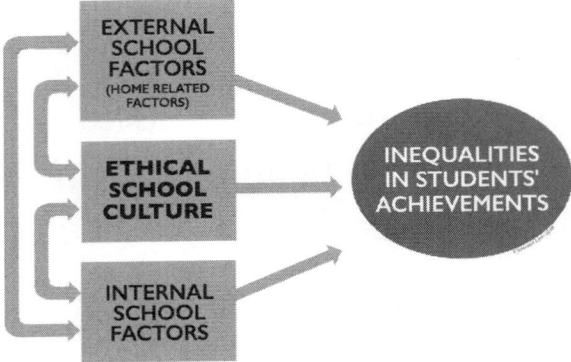

Fig. 3.1:   An Integrative Model Explaining Inequalities in Students'
Achievements (© Susannah Levin, 2018).

In this chapter, I suggest an integrative model that emphasizes how ethical school culture and the above-mentioned supposedly "distinctive" factors are intermeshed. My argument is that under various conditions, school and home factors are actually intertwined. For example, the time students spend doing homework may be affected by teachers' ethical values, norms, and beliefs. In some contexts, school decisions about class size are indeed influenced by parental pressure. Another example is the way teachers encourage after-school inquiry among students, or how principals distribute scarce school resources in case of parental intervention.

Many, if not all, of these practices entail ethical dimensions that underscore links between internal and external school factors. Thus, my approach highlights the impact of ethical school culture. This construct bridges elements both inside and outside the school that affect student achievement and may explain academic gaps and inequality among students all over the world.

To the conventional models of schooling, including external and internal school factors, I have added here the factor of ethical school culture. Although the literature has not defined ethical culture in schools, previous studies have pointed to the following four main dimensions that may characterize this concept:

1. *Caring for the students' learning and well-being*: Ethical teachers care for their students by developing their students' potential, and promoting inquiry and creativity (Joseph, 2016). Ethical teachers ensure that every student receives the highest quality of learning by helping to ensure a safe environment with fair and equitable treatment for each student (Scott, Webber, Lupart, Aitken, & Scott, 2014). These teachers create a learning environment by promoting mutual respect among teachers and their students which may promote student excellence and achievements (Koellner & Jacobs, 2015).

   When investigating the ethical aspects of students' learning, it is important to consider that countries vary based on deeply embedded cultural differences. For example, in Japan, student achievements are attributed to hard work, perseverance, and effort; in the United States, such achievements are typically attributed to intelligence, ability, and talent (Fukushima, Sharp, & Kobayashi, 2009). In France, however, teachers emphasize their overarching responsibility by providing experiences and opportunities for less advantaged students, which are similar to those experiences and opportunities enjoyed by more advantaged children (Brennan, Kavita, & Winnie, 2009).

2. *The teaching profession*: Ethical teachers base their practice on continuous professional learning and teach up-to-date subjects (Louws, Meirink, van Veen, & van Driel, 2018). These teachers know their subject matter, and use a range of strategies and assessments to teach their students, which may promote their students' achievements (Ronfeldt, Farmer, McQueen, & Grissom, 2015).

   When discussing the issue of ethical aspects of the teaching profession, it is important to be aware of the fact that different educational settings promote the teaching profession and teacher solidarity in different ways (Shapira-Lishchinsky, 2013a, 2013b). For example, teachers in Japan work together in preparing their lesson plans and didactic materials, and are provided considerable time to complete these tasks. Teachers' personal workspaces are often organized in a "bullpen" arrangement to promote professional interactions. In the United States, teachers collaborate much less frequently, although more often than in France, where secondary school teachers are viewed as autonomous professionals, and are not required to be physically present in the school unless they are teaching a class (Senk et al., 2012). Thus, the presence of collaborative cultures in school varies substantially from country to country, based, in part, on conceptions of appropriate models of teacher professionalism (Sachs, 2016).

3. *School community*: Many studies emphasize that parents' involvement and teachers' collaboration with parents directly affect student achievements (Castro et al., 2015; Jeynes, 2015; Wilder, 2014) and school effectiveness (Weiss, Lopez, & Rosenberg, 2010). The motivation to collaborate is derived from a "student-centered" attitude that parents and teachers should collaborate since they share a responsibility to promote opportunities and learning processes (Minke, Sheridan, Kim, Ryoo, & Koziol, 2014). However, by encouraging parents' involvement and teachers' collaboration with parents, ethical aspects may emerge in the form of teachers' perceptions that instead of helping, parents are interfering with and disturbing their work (Addi-Raccah & Ainhoren, 2009; Shapira-Lishchinsky, 2011).

   Considering the international findings, it was noted, for example, that in Finland, one of the higher achievement countries in TIMSS, the first priority of Finnish school principals is to maintain a continuous relationship with parents. This relationship encourages a positive climate and parental engagement (Risku, Bjork, & Browne-Ferrigno, 2012). In the United States, it was found that positive relationships between schools and parents, as well as parents' involvement, contribute to reducing ethnic gaps and improving minority students' achievements (Jeynes, 2015).

4. *Collegial relationships among teachers*: Teachers collaborate with colleagues and other professionals in the interests of student learning. They share

knowledge, which may contribute to their professional development and to student achievements (Ning, Lee, & Lee, 2015). However, the interaction between the teachers themselves and other professionals may give rise to ethical dilemmas, such as whether to report misconduct among colleagues (Shapira-Lishchinsky, 2011). International aspects also play an important role. It was discovered that in Asia and Europe, high-achievement schools dedicate much more time to teachers' teamwork and corporate design than do average performing US schools (Collier, 2011). In addition, in the Netherlands, among 411 teachers from 49 primary schools, it was found that collaboration among teachers explained significant differences in students' achievements in participating schools (Doppenberg, Brok, & Bakx, 2012).

I believe that awareness of the suggested dimensions of the concept of ethical school culture presented in this chapter may help reduce the gaps between students' achievements, which may promote social justice in schools.

Chapter 4

Social Justice in Educational Systems

When educators develop and assimilate codes of ethics for educational systems, such a process can help promote social justice in schools. This chapter broadens the understanding of the concept "social justice," including ways to integrate this concept into schools.

Morality of Care and Morality of Justice

The term "ethical reasoning" describes the process by which people confront ethical dilemmas (Abdolmohammadi, Read, & Scarbrough, 2003). There are two central components of reasoning about ethical dilemmas: "morality of justice" and "morality of care." The first one – "morality of justice" – implies the person's attempt to adopt universal rules, societal rules, and individual rights. Kohlberg's (1986) well-known research is based on the "morality of justice." His framework provides three broad levels of cognitive moral development, with each one comprising two stages. Moral development involves an individual's passage between stages; the characteristics of different levels and stages are what define "moral judgment."

When considering morality of justice in schools, we can think about the importance of legitimizing rights and obligations, such as parents' and students' rights to a "good" education, and teachers' obligations to provide such an education. Thus, success is determined by quantitative attainment published in international reports such as those produced by Trends in International Mathematics and Science Study (TIMSS), and Programme for International Student Assessment (PISA), and The Organisation for Economic Co-operation and Development (Shapira-Lishchinsky, 2018a). Therefore, schools are required to employ measures that can provide evidence of the progress of students. As a result, education becomes a political issue, insofar as it requires consideration of the ways in which student achievements are monitored and controlled (Adams, 2015).

In comparison, "morality of care" reflects a less formal approach. Its focus is on the notion of providing care and on being able to decide whether a response was appropriate in a given case. "Morality of care" is a standard that allows one

International Aspects of Organizational Ethics in Educational Systems, 17–19
Copyright © 2018 by Emerald Publishing Limited
All rights of reproduction in any form reserved
doi:10.1108/978-1-78714-777-520181004

to say that a certain behavior was appropriate for a particular individual to take, but not that it would be necessarily the correct way to act for each individual in that situation. Knowing what to do involves knowing others and being connected in ways that involve both emotion and cognition (Taylor, Gilligan, & Sullivan, 1997). "Morality of care" is distinct from "morality of justice" in that it does not attempt to follow universal rules or ensure equitable treatment. Instead, it centers on responsiveness to another's needs.

Previous studies have shown that morality of care tends to be reflected in teachers' statements about professionalism, and the way in which teachers define themselves in terms of care (Shapiro & Stefkovich, 2010; Tirri & Husu, 2002). What is relevant, however, is the way in which care, as an aspect of interpersonal relationships, aligns itself with issues connected to education. Positions adopted by the psychology of morality, taking place within a caring framework, move us toward the heart of education-caring relationships with students (Adams, 2015).

According to Adams (2015), there are two main approaches to the relationship between the concepts of morality of justice and morality of care: (1) *the superiority approach* holds that one ethic is superior to the other. It is generally argued in favor of justice, although some assert that care is the superior approach. (2) *The integration approach* seeks to find one monistic theory; it asserts that care and justice are intertwined. In other words, justice cannot exist without care and vice versa. Gilligan & Attanucci (1988) saw care and justice as being intertwined: care is conceived through the prism of justice, and also offers a perspective on moral action. The researchers concluded that the perspective of justice is incomplete without an accompanying care perspective.

Social Justice in Educational Systems

When "social justice" is used in the context of educational systems, it is a very malleable expression, with numerous meanings (Boylan & Woolsey, 2015). Our understanding of social justice is rooted in the importance of adopting both distributive and relational perspective as well as recognizing that it has a participative dimension (Fraser, 2009).

The *distributive aspect* refers to the significance of equitable access to educational goods and outcomes. *Socially just relationality* includes the recognition of, and respect for, social and cultural differences. Finally, the participative dimension addresses the capacity and opportunity to be an active participant in decision making (Cochran-Smith, 2009). Given that social justice is enacted in and through embodied relationships, it is paramount to pay attention to social and macro issues, including school organization and societal outcomes. However, it is no less important to consider personal and micro issues as well as the interplay between them (North, 2008).

Ways to Promote Social Justice in Educational Systems

Whereas contemporary approaches for the promotion of social justice are impacted by a diverse array of educational, philosophical, and political movements, social justice is heavily based on the following three pedagogical philosophies: democratic education, critical pedagogy, and culturally responsive education (Dewey, 2007). Education that is *democratic* includes the teaching of skills that are necessary for the promotion of civic participation. Most educators who follow such an approach see students' responsibility for their actions as being a key; they engage in active participation in a school-based society as well as in an out-of-school society. Finally, they express agency when promoting societal change (Westheimer & Kahne, 2004).

Critical pedagogy challenges the political neutrality of the curricula, pedagogy, and educational systems. This type of pedagogy aspires to develop students' sociopolitical consciousness by engaging them in co-investigation, the posing of problems, and ongoing dialogue. Critical pedagogy avers that it is essential to analyze the existing relationships between sociopolitical power, social processes, and the construction of knowledge. It needs to reflect on sociocultural realities and take ownership over class processes and products (Duncan-Andrade & Morrell, 2008).

Culturally responsive education concentrates on teachers' identities and students' academic achievements. Specifically, culturally responsive educators assert that it is extremely important to analyze the political ideologies of teachers, their preparation before they begin teaching, their technical skills, and their willingness to work for change. These educators aver that teachers must undergo training that readies them to work for the minimization of social and educational inequity (González, Moll, & Amanti, 2005). Culturally responsive teachers also understand the significance of their students' lives and experiences outside the school, family structures, interests, beliefs about schooling, and the demographic, religious, and sociopolitical context of the community in which they teach (Dover, 2013).

Its appears that these three pedagogical philosophies can promote the development of codes for teachers by training them to be active members of their communities, by encouraging civic participation, challenging the political neutrality of curriculum, and reducing social and educational inequity.

Chapter 5

Cross-National Aspects: The Process of Developing a Code of Ethics

In order to promote social justice and ethical culture in educational systems, educational leadership should encourage the development of codes of ethics and work toward assimilating them into the system and conserving them. However, we should be aware that these activities take a long time. For many years, there has been an ongoing process of developing a code of ethics for the teaching profession. In Ireland, for example, it took a decade from the beginning until the final document was published. In Hong Kong, the process took eight years, and in Israel, while the process began in 1978 with the Etzioni Report, it has not yet ended. As a result, when beginning to develop a code of ethics, the participants in the process need to be aware that its professional and deep development takes place in stages, in which each stage undergoes inspection and approval before the process can move on to the next stage, and that the final product will take years. For example, in countries such as Ireland, Canada, England, Korea, Australia, Hong Kong, New Zealand, and the United States, at least two versions of the codes of ethics were developed and approved by the authorities until they reached their final form.

Different stages in the development of a code of ethics are detailed as follows.

The First Stage: Awareness of the Importance of the Process

It is important that educational leaders responsible for developing the code of ethics be aware of the importance of the code. It needs to be seen as an instrument of professional empowerment for educators and the teaching profession that leads to quality teaching, excellence in education via the promotion of learning and a learning environment, and the promotion of joint ethical values by educators and teachers (Shapira-Lishchinsky, 2011).

The advantage of creating such a code is that it provides a clear framework of the rules that explains the expected ethical behavior of the teacher. The code of ethics presents desirable and valued behavior; it also facilitates arriving at daily ethical decisions. Furthermore, it trains teachers in desirable behavior

International Aspects of Organizational Ethics in Educational Systems, 21–26
Copyright © 2018 by Emerald Publishing Limited
All rights of reproduction in any form reserved
doi:10.1108/978-1-78714-777-520181005

(Shapira-Lishchinsky, 2013a). The constructors of the codes expect that these rules will increase the trust of the public in the educational system and the educators, the agents of the system (Poisson, 2009). Nevertheless, it is important to note that while the ethical code can be helpful, it does not provide a clear definition for each and every situation, since it is impossible to define every possible ethical situation. Therefore, ethical knowledge, skills, and the possibility of practicing different situations and responding to them are needed when dealing with ethical dilemmas that can lead to empowerment of educators (Maynard & Burke, 2015).

The Second Stage: Choosing the Committee Members Who Will Lead the Process

All staff members who wish to promote human resources in the organization by developing a code of ethics can be included in the committee. The staff should include representatives from the Ministry of Education's headquarters, and teachers and educators who have different functions: school principals, vice principals, supervisors, counselors, representatives of teachers' organizations, and academic representatives who undertake research on organizational ethics. The committee should also include students. Development of the code of ethics by people from different professional backgrounds will, thus, include different viewpoints and deepen the quality of the development process. Committee members will be able to examine, from different viewpoints, the ethical rules that are appropriate for minimizing behavioral problems.

The Third Stage: The Process of Developing the Ethical Code

Poisson (2009) presents a helpful process for the development of a code of ethics in educational organizations. She proposes involving all of the stakeholders in order to increase obligation to the process, help when there is resistance to the process, and when there is a need to enlist economic and human resources for such a process. Afterwards, it is appropriate to choose representatives from all groups of stakeholders to be the members of the *main working group*, which will prepare the draft proposal. For this work, it is recommended to use codes of ethics that have been developed in other educational organizations of the world and in organizations that are not connected to education; ethical events from the field; school ethical standards, which were developed in the past; and theses and dissertations that address ethical dilemmas connected to education. All these can be used in brainstorming sessions and they can offer additional ideas for development of the statements in the ethical codes.

When working on the draft and the final versions, globally it is customary for the code to begin with a customary declaration. The ethical rules of behavior are then formulated. Globally, there are different ways to formulate codes of ethics for educators and teachers. Some of them are written in the imperative, for example: "The teacher should..." Others are written by an educator in the first person, for example: "I will work to promote..." The phrasing should be positive, one that encourages the teacher's inner motivation; for example, using the phrase: "I believe...," instead of using an imperative: "the educator/teacher should..." At the end of the document, it is appropriate to include a declaration signed by the educator/teacher, stating that s/he has read the document and agrees with the code.

As noted above, the process of developing a code of ethics has a number of steps. At each stage, the drafts change. In different countries (e.g., in Ireland and England), when the code of ethics was developed in the first stage, after the committee or the council that had been authorized to create the code had worked on it, the draft ("Document draft I") was sent to the *advisory committee*, which also comprised stakeholders, such as those described above. However, this group comprised of different people, who gave their feedback. Based on the draft, the advisory committee undertook focus group interviews and attended school meetings with stakeholders, including groups that were perceived as suffering from discrimination in the educational system. This helped the drafters remain aware of all possible ethical aspects that were important to improve the code. Following are the examples of questions for evaluation of the "Draft document I": "What did you like/dislike in the proposed code of ethics?" and "What would you add/delete from the proposed code?" The proposal and the corrections for improvement were then sent back to the main working group.

It is important to note that though it appears that the advisory committee complicates and extends the process, this committee is designed to be the "watchdog" of the process. For example, in the proposed code, it can ask whether the voice of the Ministry of Education is the only voice heard. Afterwards, the committee or the council, described above, prepares a revised document ("Draft document II"), according to the recommendations of the advisory committee. Then this revised document is sent to the different circles of educational community (different levels of schools, different sectors, the headquarters of the Ministry of Education, and the educational authorities). The document is discussed in group meetings in order to receive additional feedback. After this round, the final document has received approval from the bodies with the authority to demand that the educational system adopts it, and even to impose sanctions if an educator and/or teacher does not work according to the code of ethics.

The Fourth Stage: Assimilation of the Code of Ethics

As noted above, after the relevant authorities have agreed that the code is valid, and they commit to enforcing and supporting it through the law, different educational systems in the world have worked at distributing it via e-mail, social media, and in posters distributed to schools and to teachers' organizations. In addition, workshops for assimilation of the code have been developed for teachers. Application of the code has used the investigation of ethical events, different strategies for the treatment of complaints, and the determining and application of sanctions (e.g., giving a warning, suspension, or dismissal) by the committee that was given the authority to develop the code by the State.

It is important to also remember that in countries in which a code of ethics was developed, there have been numerous cases in which the teachers were unaware that such a code existed. Furthermore, educators and teachers have had a hard time understanding the connections to the field and the leaders of the code have lacked knowledge about how to enforce the code (Poisson, 2009). Therefore, it is recommended, for assimilation of the code, to construct experiential workshops that will leave their mark on the participants (Shapira-Lishchinsky, 2013a).

The Fifth Stage: Feedback and Supervision of the Process

When examining the codes of ethics that have been developed in the world, it was found that after the first draft of the code was presented, it took between three and five years, on the average, until the revised version was presented. This second draft had undergone changes based on feedback from the field concerning the original version and the political and technological changes that had occurred over time. These changes raise new ethical challenges and demand additional tools for dealing with them. During the supervision and feedback process, it is worthwhile to provide responses to these questions: Are the codes that were developed clear? To what extent did the developed codes advance the teaching profession? What changes should be made to the code of ethics? How many educators and teachers have signed the code? Do all the stakeholders have access to the ethical code?

In Table 5.1, the processes of development of an ethical code for educators and the teaching profession from three countries, which were randomly selected, are presented. The information in the table relates to the code title, the rationale for the code's development, its goals, the body given the authority to develop the ethical code, how the process is led, the validity process for the enforcement of the code, how the supervision process works, the potential impact of the ethical code, and the question whether the code relates to the issue of enforcement and imposing of sanctions.

Awareness of the processes of development and application of an ethical code for educators and the teaching profession, from different randomly selected countries, can be helpful for the design and application while eliciting ideas to develop new codes and updating the existing ones.

Table 5.1: The Process of Development and Application of Ethical Codes: Slovenia, the United States, and Thailand.

Country	Code title	Structure	Goals	Process	Confirmed by	Impact	Sanctions
Slovenia	Code of Ethics for members of the Association of Slovenian Catholic Teachers	Items are organized according to four categories: (1) Respect of students' rights; (2) Respect of family rights; (3) Protection of the school's integrity; (4) Protection of the status of teaching profession	Guidance, support, encouragement, provision of a framework, inspiration, commitment, and accountability for behaving according to ethical norms	The draft was ratified at the annual general meeting of the Association in 1997. The revised and completed version passed the association's annual general meeting in 2005	The Association of Slovenian Catholic Teachers	The code impacted teachers and educators, including Slovenian teachers in neighboring countries and in Argentina	Violations of the code are addressed by the Association's honor tribunal
USA	The Association of American Educators (AAE) Code of Ethics for Educators	The items are organized according to four categories: Ethical conduct: (1) Toward students; (2) Toward practices and performance; (3) Toward professional colleagues; (4) Toward parents and the community	(1) Creating an environment that can fulfill the potential of all students. (2) Illustrating the highest ethical standards. (3) Acceptance of the fact that every child has a right to an uninterrupted education (free from strikes)	Drafted by a distinguished group of educators from the AAE Advisory Board and Executive Committee in 1994	The AAE Advisory Board	The code was constructed around the rights of students and educators	No response

Table 5.1:   *(Continued)*

Country	Code title	Structure	Goals	Process	Confirmed by	Impact	Sanctions
Thailand	Regulation of the Teachers' Council of Thailand on professional standards and ethics (2005)	The items are organized in three categories: (1) Standards of professional knowledge and experience; (2) Performance standards; (3) Professional ethics	Acting according to ethical guidelines to promote education	There are four main steps: (1) Paragraph 1 (11) (e), (f) of Sections 9, 49, and 50 of the Teachers and Educational Personnel Council Act B.E. 2546 (2003); (2) Teachers' Council of Thailand Board Meeting No. 9/2005 on June 20, 2005; (3) Teachers' Council of Thailand Board Meeting No. 10/2005 on July 18, 2005 (4) Approval of the Minister of Education and the Teachers' Council of Thailand Board	The Teachers' Council of Thailand's Board	Administrators, educational administrators, and other educational personnel who are granted licenses to practice under the Teachers and Educational Personnel Council Act	The chairperson of the Board of the Teachers' Council governs execution of the regulation and has the power to issue rules that ensure that professionals obey the regulations

Chapter 6

Ensuring Assimilation of the Code of Ethics: A Cross-National View

As presented in the previous chapters, most countries refer to the teaching profession when developing their codes of ethics for their educational systems. My approach is that we should encourage the development of codes of ethics for all stakeholders, including school principals, based on the fact that principals experience similar ethical challenges to those of teachers. It is worthwhile to consider their unique ethical challenges in the appendices of the code. Based on this understanding, this chapter discusses the assimilation of the code of ethics in the educational system by educational leaders and teachers.

The effective way to ensure assimilation of ethical codes is through educational processes that lead educational leaders and teachers to become aware of the importance of the ethical code for the promotion of an ethical environment in schools. If educational leaders and teachers are unaware of the importance of improving the school's atmosphere and teachers' professional skills, the development of procedures and sanctions against actions that do not meet the ethical code will lead the teachers to hide their unacceptable behavior, but not to decrease it.

The importance of having mechanisms for supervision and enforcement will be understood when and if the assimilation processes become sensitive processes based on the use of pedagogical means. In addition, teachers, who are aware of the ways to enforce the rules and impose sanctions, will behave in accordance with the code due to their fear of sanctions. However, at the same time, they will also try to understand the reasons for the procedures. Understanding the motivations can help encourage teachers to act accordingly in the future, as they develop inner motivations to behave in ethical ways, and not because of a sanction. In any event, the sanctions and enforcement of the code need to be meted out in a fair and proportional manner and match the level of unethical behavior in order to create trust in the code of ethics.

Throughout the world, there are different ways to supervise and enforce the ethical codes that have been developed (Poisson, 2009). These ways include the following:

International Aspects of Organizational Ethics in Educational Systems, 27–28
Copyright © 2018 by Emerald Publishing Limited
All rights of reproduction in any form reserved
doi:10.1108/978-1-78714-777-520181006

- In the code itself, it is relevant to clearly detail the ways in which unacceptable behavior will be reported, and the sanctions for violations. These need to be clearly communicated to the teachers and to the school principals (e.g., sending emails or a phone number of the person in charge of the supervisory process). This will make it possible for educational leaders and teachers to report unacceptable behavior and to continue supervision in a discreet manner. It is important to note that the reporting of extreme unacceptable behaviors, which contradict the ethical code, is obligatory and is not left to the discretion of educational leaders and teachers (similar to the cases of sexual harassment, drug use, fraud concerning an earned degree, etc.). Educational leaders and teachers need to know to whom to report so that the issue can be addressed and people will be able to access the relevant authority. In this way, the treatment will not solely serve as a response for educators and teachers, but will also be a response for all stakeholders, such as the school's administration and community, which includes students, their parents, and the workers in the educational system.
- The committee responsible for dealing with unethical events needs to handle the complaints in a timely fashion. It is recommended that representatives from the teachers' organizations participate in these committees, either as members or as observers. This can help prevent making decisions that *only* guide policy. The presence of representatives can also help maintain the balance between the decision-making process and the teachers' interests.
- This committee collects relevant data in the field that connects the event. They do this via interviews and through an investigation of the event in the school, exploring everything connected to the incident. It prepares the report that outlines the facts, the investigative process and its findings, and proposes clear recommendations concerning possible sanctions. If the committee decides that a sanction is in order, it recommends what sanctions should be applied. These actions are undertaken while safeguarding the teacher's status and rights, his/her full access to the evidence, and ensuring that the teacher can defend him/herself and be protected by representatives that s/he chooses. The process safeguards the stakeholders' rights to obtain the decision in writing, the reasons for the decision as well as the right to submit an appeal to the authoritative body.
- Accepted sanctions imposed by committees in the world include the following: disciplinary comments, warnings, fines, transferring a teacher/administrator from a school, reproach/censure, or revoking a teacher's license, an act made known to the public.

Chapter 7

Codes of Ethics as Promoting Teachers' Professional Status

Previous studies have shown that developing and assimilating codes of ethics for teachers can aid in the promotion of the profession (Campbell, 2000; Maxwell & Schwimmer, 2016). This is because the codes recommend certain behaviors which can help teachers learn how to handle ethical challenges in appropriate manner. The codes also help define teachers' roles. Therefore, these mechanisms have the potential of increasing teachers' professionalism (Shapira-Lishchinsky, 2009b, 2013a, 2013b). High standards of ethics are considered to be signs of professionalism and are also necessary for acquiring a high status of professionalism (Strike & Soltis, 2015).

When looking at the parallels between teaching and other professions, it is worthwhile to examine the following three criteria: (a) the mystification of knowledge; (b) social distance; and (c) reciprocity of effort (Richardson & Fenstermacher, 2001).

Mystification of knowledge refers to the teachers' responsibility to work with their students on the acquisition of knowledge. This is not something that other professionals necessarily view as part of their roles (e.g., engineers).

Social distance refers to the close relationships teachers must create with their students in order to understand what their students' lives are like. This differs from many other professions in which the creation of close relationships is not essential, thus making it possible to maintain a social distance (e.g., lawyers).

Reciprocity of effort refers to the fact that in teaching both sides (i.e., students and teachers) work to achieve satisfactory results. In many professions, results can beachieved when one side (e.g., the client) does not make any effort to improve the situation (Colnerud, 2006).

Teachers have long struggled to raise their professional status (Mausethagen & Granlund, 2012). Unfortunately, teachers have always suffered from a problematic professional status when compared to highly regarded professions, such as medicine and law. One particular issue that is an evidence of the relatively low status of teaching is that teacher education is seen as a poorly esteemed profession

International Aspects of Organizational Ethics in Educational Systems, 29–31
Copyright © 2018 by Emerald Publishing Limited
All rights of reproduction in any form reserved
doi:10.1108/978-1-78714-777-520181007

(Monteiro, 2015). In addition, teachers tend to be underpaid and overworked. This makes it difficult for colleges and universities to recruit good teachers for students' education (Aslan & Bakir, 2017). As a result, the teaching profession continues to lose prestige. In turn, this leads to more and more competent teachers leaving the profession after having taught for only a few years (Harfitt, 2015; Struyven & Vanthournout, 2014).

In general, there is consensus that professions share certain characteristics. These characteristics are as follows: (1) mastery of a body of knowledge and skills to be applied to the profession; (2) an orientation toward communal service; (3) a distinct professional code of ethics that is formulated in a code of practice. This justifies the profession to regulate itself; and (4) a built-in comparison with other occupations. This highlights the autonomy and prestige of the profession (Carr, 2005).

In many countries such as the United States (Zeichner & Pena-Sandoval, 2015), Australia (Mayer, 2014), Canada (Darling-Hammond, 2017), Sweden (Samuelsson & Lindblad, 2015), the United Kingdom (Lindqvist, Nordänger, & Carlsson, 2014), Germany (Henoch, Klusmann, Lüdtke, & Trautwein, 2015), France (Page, 2015), and Israel (Shapira-Lishchinsky 2009b), teaching has not shared most of these characteristics. In these countries, the body of knowledge that college students acquire in teacher education, for example, has not been seen as sufficiently unique to the profession. Furthermore, countries do not permit sufficient self-regulation. Finally, the relative autonomy and prestige in education have not matched the independence and prestige found in other established professions (for example, in medicine and law).

Teachers face complex situations in which their status, facilities, and/or knowledge provide sufficient support (Schleicher, 2015). Strengthening teacher competency, in addition to providing required knowledge and skills, can help promote a commitment to increase professional and ethical standards on the part of teachers (He & Van De Vijver, 2015; Maxwell & Schwimmer, 2016).

Promotion of Teachers' Professional Status Through Ethical Knowledge

Ajzen and Fishbein's (2005) theory asserts that perceptions lead to behaviors. Research has shown that people who face ethical dilemmas in different manners also differ predictably in their perceptions (Shapiro & Stefkovich, 2016). If we apply this theory to teachers' professional and organizational ethics, it can be expected that ethical knowledge will enlarge and deepen the ethical perceptions of educators (Niemi, Toom, & Kallioniemi, 2016). This, in turn, may lead to more effective resolution of ethical dilemmas. The reasoning is that ethical knowledge enables teachers to conceptually and practically link core values, such as fairness and respect for others, together with their own nuanced choices and actions. This may move teachers beyond their technical and disciplinary ability, leading them to appreciate the potential formal and informal ethical impact their practice can have on their students (Campbell, 2012).

The ability to discuss ethical perceptions may also help teachers better understand their professional responsibilities and the limits of these obligations (Tellez, 2016). The development of educational programs, rooted in creating and integrating codes of ethics for teachers, which stress the need to deal with ethical implications of daily interactions, has the potential to increase teachers' knowledge and the ability of teachers to successfully cope with ethical dilemmas (Cameron & O'Leary, 2015). As a result, this may raise the professional status of teaching both in the teachers' eyes and in the eyes of the community as well (Braun, 2015). Fig. 7.1 demonstrates this process.

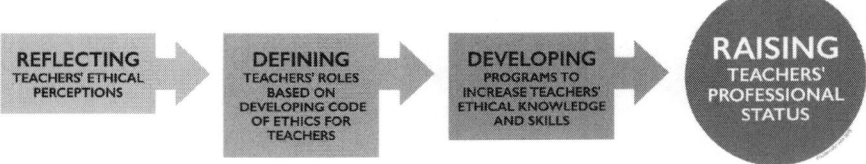

Fig. 7.1:   The Ethical Aspects of Teachers' Professionalism
(© Susannah Levin, 2018).

Chapter 8

The US Code of Ethics for Educators: A Case Study

The United States is perceived as being a huge power; therefore, it is interesting to examine how codes of ethics have been developed in such a large system. This exploration makes it possible for us to learn from successes and failures of the American educational system while remaining aware of the cultural and political differences connected to leading a similar process in other countries.

In the United States, ethical codes, or standards of professional behavior, have been developed by professional committees that were authorized by the different departments of education in states such as Oklahoma, New Jersey, Mississippi, Idaho, Arkansas, Colorado, Kentucky, Florida, Oregon, and in conjunction with universities such as in New York. Simultaneously, a code of ethics has been developed by the National Education Association – to which most of the teachers in the country belong – and a separate ethical code has been developed by the smaller and competing organization – the American Association of Educators (AAE).

While teachers' associations have chosen to develop ethical rules for educators and teachers that work throughout the United States, different states, with the aid of their departments of education, have chosen to develop their own codes for their educators and teachers. The educational system in the United States is decentralized and run by each state. In other words, each state has the autonomy to shape its own educational policy. We can ask whether there is justification for having separate ethical codes in each state and a separate code for the teachers' organizations noted above. Furthermore, we can see whether their contents differ from one another.

I will begin by addressing the following question: Why the two teachers' associations have their own codes of ethics? The National Educational Association is a senior teachers' organization. In contrast, the AAE is a relatively new organization that was established with the desire to emphasize a different vision and perception of how the teaching profession should be shaped in terms of the interaction of the teachers with students, colleagues, parents, and the community.

International Aspects of Organizational Ethics in Educational Systems, 33–35
Copyright © 2018 by Emerald Publishing Limited
All rights of reproduction in any form reserved
doi:10.1108/978-1-78714-777-520181008

As a result, each association possesses a different model of the teaching profession, which finds expression in its code of ethics.

It was found that while the ethical code of the National Educational Association focuses on the obligations toward the students and the profession, the AAE focuses on the following four main categories: (a) ethical behavior toward students, (b) ethical behavior toward praxis and performance, (c) ethical behavior toward colleagues, and (d) ethical behavior toward parents and the community. As a result, it appears as if the younger association expands the understanding of the profession concerning characteristics of ethical behavior of teachers. However, both codes, first and foremost, express their concern for both the student and the teaching profession. Furthermore, these codes do not relate to enforcement or use of sanctions against teachers who engage in unethical behaviors.

However, it was found that most of the ethical codes that were developed in the US states *do* relate to the enforcement process and imposing of sanctions. These states created ethical codes that are legal documents, written as commands or directives. For example, the Teacher Standards and Practices Commission from Oregon, the Educator Code of Ethics from Alabama, the Code of Ethics for Educators from Georgia, the Teachers' Code of Ethics from Colorado, the Educator Code of Ethics and Standards of Conduct from Mississippi, and the Standards of Performance and Conduct for Teachers from Oklahoma, are written in such a manner.

In other states, while the ethical code is written as a command or directive, the code does not relate to sanctions or to enforcement of the code. Examples of these include the Code of Ethics and Standard Practices for Texas Educators, the Code of Ethics of the Tennesse Education Association, the Professional Educators of Montana Code of Ethics, and the Code of Professional Conduct for Educators from North Dakota.

In the other states, the code provides general terms concerning the expected standards in the teaching profession. This is found, for example, in the New York State Code of Ethics for Educators, the Code of Professional Practice and Conduct for Educators from Pennsylvania, Michigan's Professional Educator's Code of Ethics, and the Code of Ethics for Vermont Educators: A Statement of Beliefs. In these states, there is no mention of use of sanctions or enforcement. New York explicitly states in its code of ethics that it should *not* be used as a basis for sanctions when there are disciplinary problems or instances of unacceptable behavior.

It is also important to note the titles of the codes of ethics in different states to illustrate the varied approaches to the codes. Some of the states solely relate to the code of ethics in their titles; some of them interweave the code of ethics with behavioral rules or expected standards from the teachers; and some only note in the title that the document relates to expected standards and behavioral rules for educators and teachers, without explicitly mentioning that the document addresses rules of ethical behavior. Nevertheless, it is clear that all of the states expect teachers to behave ethically and that this is an inseparable part of the standards and the expected rules of behavior in general. Most of the states relate to the following four ethical dimensions, regardless whether the document is written in legal terms or as a document that defines what is expected from the

the teachers and the teaching profession: obligation to the student, obligation to the profession, obligation to one's colleagues, and obligations to the parents and the community. These dimensions are explicit: these are either divided into these categories in the code itself, or can be discerned from the statements.

At the beginning of the chapter, I asked whether there was justification for each state and for the two teachers' associations to develop separate ethical codes. The same basic spirit of the ethical code, whether developed by a state or a teacher's organization, can be found in all the documents. To begin with, the standards of upholding an obligation to provide quality education and to promote the teaching profession are interwoven with one another. It appears that in order to achieve better assimilation of the ethical code and the obligation of the educators and teachers in the United States, it would have been better if one code had been jointly developed by the different departments of education and the teachers' associations, rather than separately by each body. It is possible that the development of separate codes by the different departments of education and teachers' associations explain why many school principals, teachers, and researchers of education in the United States are unaware of these ethical codes.

Chapter 9

The Hidden "Ethical School Culture" Factor in the TIMSS International Assessment: An Updated Study

One of the goals of the International Association for the Evaluation of Educational Achievement's (IEA) Trends in International Mathematics and Science Study (TIMSS) is to promote equity policies that aim to minimize achievement gaps and reduce the differences in test scores between higher and lower scoring groups (Mullis, Martin, Foy, & Hooper, 2016). Furthermore, countries that participate in the design of educational policies pay attention to equity issues by using examples, such as promoting the potential of students by maximizing the performance of students who do not show achievements (Hanushek & Woessmann, 2015). The ethical context found in TIMSS reports (Mullis, Martin, & Loveles, 2016; in addition to analyzing different codes of ethics in order to elicit the meaning of ethical school culture; see Chapter 2), encouraged me to compare 45 countries that participated in the TIMSS, in order to elicit the concept of ethical school culture.

TIMSS 2015 continued a 20-year international assessment of achievements in math and science, conducted by the IEA, among school principals, teachers, and students. The IEA is an independent international cooperative comprising national research institutions and government agencies. Data for the research came from questionnaires that were completed by 8,353 teachers nested in 8,353 schools from 45 countries. I mainly focused on the teachers' challenges, satisfaction, professional development, and teaching experiences. Mplus software was used for exploratory and confirmatory factoring analysis (Muthén & Muthén, 2017).

The study (Shapira-Lishchinsky, 2018a) offers additional meaning to the TIMSS questionnaires completed by the teachers since the analysis expose a new factor – "ethical school culture" – that finds agreement among experts in ethics in education in different countries. The analysis of the data provided a deeper cross-national meaning for "ethical school culture," since it led to the identification of four dimensions of this concept: "teachers' profession," "care for students'

International Aspects of Organizational Ethics in Educational Systems, 37–38
doi:10.1108/978-1-78714-777-520181009

learning," "interaction with colleagues," and "respect of rules." These dimensions are similar to the ethical dimensions that emerged in the analyses of the codes of ethics for teachers and educators in different countries (see Chapter 2).

The first dimension, *teachers' profession*, includes aspects of professional standards. Examples are: conducting science experiments, adapting teaching, evaluating students, and using the method of inquiry. The second dimension, *care for students' learning*, comprises aspects of support provided to teachers by the school leadership or the school leadership that supports the professional development of teachers. The third dimension, *interaction with colleagues*, includes discussions of how to teach and the joint sharing of teaching experiences between peers. The fourth dimension, *respect of rules*, covers the rules to be enforced and provide clear rules about proper student conduct.

In other words, while the TIMSS developers did not intend to develop the concept of "ethical school culture" based on teachers' responses to the questionnaires, the research showed that the concept of "ethical school culture" exhibited high internal reliability for the proposed dimensions of "ethical school culture."

The above-noted dimensions, which were identified in the teachers' TIMSS questionnaires, can help us understand what should be done in order to promote ethical culture in schools. Promoting such a culture has the potential to reduce achievement gaps between students. Furthermore, it can encourage the creation of an atmosphere of psychological support among teachers and students, thus reflecting ethical values in schools.

Section II

International Aspects of Ethics and Leadership

Chapter 10

Ethical Aspects of Educational Leadership and Training

In the following chapters, I will focus on organizational ethical aspects of educational leadership and preparation of educational leadership. As Astin and Astin (2000) and Bogotch (2000) clearly remind us that leadership is deeply rooted in moral and ethical values in a social context. Our societies have expectations that school leaders will arrive at ethical decisions (Starratt, 2007) and that the motivations behind their behaviors will be driven by a commitment to moral excellence. Shields (2010) proposed that while educators must balance numerous demands, which often compete with one another for time and resources, educational leaders must give ample time and place to facilitate moral dialogue. Such a dialogue can open up doors in schools for the students of the community to have an educational experience that is socially just and deeply democratic.

Thus, today, parents and teachers expect educational leaders to engage in processes of ethical decision making, whether working alone or with others in teams, which is characteristic of the way most of today's school leadership activities are carried out (Branson & Gross, 2014; Shapiro & Stefkovich, 2016). As educational leaders must often deal with dynamic circumstances that are characterized by stress and ambiguity, personal attributes, such as the ability to establish positive interpersonal relations during teamwork and to engage in an ethical decision-making process, are essential for planning and running educational institutions (Gross & Shapiro, 2015).

The international literature has tended to perceive the school principal as a moral agent (Greenfield, 2004; Roach, Smith, & Boutin, 2011). Furthermore, the school principal is seen as being *the* moral authority, that is, the person ultimately accountable for happenings in the school (Sergiovanni, 1996). However, as research has uncovered, school principals do not appear to be sufficiently aware of the moral impact of their behaviors (Campbell, 2000; Husu & Tirri, 2003; Thornberg, 2008). These results have led educational philosophers, who study moral dilemmas facing leaders, to aver that there is a pressing need to develop awareness of principals concerning the many ethical dilemmas they will face and to provide them with the tools to suitably cope with them, when the dilemmas arise (Colnerud, 2006).

International Aspects of Organizational Ethics in Educational Systems, 41–42
Copyright © 2018 by Emerald Publishing Limited
doi:10.1108/978-1-78714-777-520181010

All this means that in order for educators to be prepared for successfully maintaining careers in school leadership, it is essential that they undergo training in dealing with ethical dilemmas, including working as teams under stressful conditions (Begley & Johansson, 2006). Unfortunately, this professional wish has yet to be realized. Owing to financial or time limitations, lack of professional interest, or shortcomings in schools' curricula, many people, who have trained to become principals, graduate from leadership programs without undergoing sufficient training for dealing with ethical dilemmas that arise in schools (Stefkovich & Begley, 2007). As a result, there is a real need to dedicate resources to help leaders develop their potential to cope effectively with ethical problems. Moreover, it is important that such support begins during the training stage, before the future principals find themselves in real-time situations in which unethical decisions or actions can seriously harm their schools (Begley & Stefkovich, 2007).

There are a number of important studies that have emphasized the need for including ethics in educational leadership programs. For example, Davis, Darling-Hammond, LaPointe, and Meyerson (2005) highlighted the need for candidates in leadership programs to grapple with real-world dilemmas as they attempt to reach good decisions through an ethical process. Other researchers, Young, Crow, Orr, Ogawa, and Creighton (2005), emphasized the importance of curricula in leadership programs to include numerous hours devoted to ethical deliberations faced by educational leadership. Research has also pointed to the expectation that educational administrators are morally obligated to serve as public educators and to develop ethical schools (Shapiro & Stefkovich, 2010). Perhaps the strongest indication of the demand for ethical behavior and decision-making can be seen in the choice made by the Educational Leadership Constituent Council (National Policy Board for Educational Administration, 2002). This board chose ethics, integrity, and fairness as independent standards to which every leadership program should aspire. In short, all of the above clearly demonstrate the need to develop moral leadership among candidates for the position of school principal.

Chapter 11

Ethical Aspects of Transactional, Transformational, and Authentic Leadership Styles

In this chapter, I present different styles of leadership that reflect ethical meaning while focusing on authentic leadership, which focuses mainly on ethical aspects.

The first leadership style, *transactional leadership,* can be defined as "relationships of exchange"; in other words, this is a system of rewards and goals. This leadership style sets school goals that teachers should achieve, and rewards the educators according to their achievements vis-à-vis those goals (Shields, 2010). Transactional leadership includes an ethical meaning, since it takes into account the fact that teachers expect to receive fair rewards for their efforts.

The second leadership style is termed as *transformational leadership*. This style articulates a complex vision of the future. It is one that can be shared with peers and subordinates, it intellectually stimulates subordinates, and it pays attention to individual differences between people (Orphanos & Orr, 2014). The ethical meaning of transformational leadership is derived from research that perceived transformational leaders as moral agents, who not only lead their staffs but also offer support and treat each employee as unique. Furthermore, such leaders encourage the creation of a climate in which people can express their beliefs and values (e.g., Kanungo, 2001).

The third leadership style is termed as *authentic leadership*. This is leadership that reflects an awareness of the way leaders think and act and are understood by others. Authentic leaders promote the expression of diverse viewpoints and create networks of collaborative relationships among the workers for whom they are responsible (Avolio, 2007). The ethical meaning of authentic leadership is reflected by the leader's own high moral attitude, and that of his/her followers, toward making an effort within and outside the organization (Begley, 2006). Starratt (2004) noted that every individual possesses the "virtue of authenticity," and it is through this virtue that people can realize their potential. The virtue of authenticity has three aspects. The *self* carries an implicit moral imperative to be true to oneself. This can only be discovered, defined, and actualized by the individual. The component, *relations*, refers to the fact that authenticity can only

International Aspects of Organizational Ethics in Educational Systems, 43–45
doi:10.1108/978-1-78714-777-520181011

truly be realized in relationships with others. When people enter into dialogue with another, and interact with one another's culture, this teaches the individual extremely important moral lessons about life. *Freedom* is the third aspect, and this reflects the individual's freedom to choose and shape one's life. This aspect reflects the fact that a person can only truly be free in a society that worries about and guarantees freedom for all.

The authentic leader's work has its basis in authenticity. It calls on teachers to be true to what they profess, to interact with students in an authentic manner, and to create educational programs that result in authentic learning (Begley, 2006). It is also expected that the educational leader will make demands of the students; s/he will strongly encourage them to assume responsibility in the community, and to help with the co-creation of a school in which there is authentic learning in order to turn the school into a place that offers a space for practicing civic responsibilities (Starratt, 2005). Consequently, authentic leadership cannot grow in a vacuum; it is dependent on the context, which includes the school and the society of the leaders (Starratt, 2007). This context is characterized by a multifaceted and dynamic synthesis of a person's values, society's fundamental values, and many other features that influence leadership (e.g., policy, politics, etc.) as well as the organizational environment (Walker & Shuangye, 2007).

As a result, we can define authentic leadership in education as a combination of ethical leadership practices and moral literacy relevant for school leaders (Begley & Stefkovich, 2007). Having knowledge of one's self and being sensitive to others create authentic leadership (Begley, 2001, 2003). This phenomenon is generally thought of as being true to oneself (Wang & Bird, 2011). An authentic leader can become an ethical leader when she/he demonstrates a high moral attitude and encourages and supports moral behavior among people on his/her staff. Furthermore, there is a real attempt to behave in meaningful ways inside and outside the organization (Begley, 2006). As Avolio noted (2007), authentic leadership is essential for the production and sustainment of the effective leadership required to create ethical and trustworthy work environments.

Begley (2001, 2006) stressed the effectiveness of authentic leadership in educational practice. In his approach, authentic leadership combines a number of aspects. It is the outcome of self-knowledge, it reflects sensitivity to the orientations of others, and it demonstrates technical sophistication that leads to a synergy of leadership action. Begley (2006) viewed authentic leadership as a relevant way to conceptualize processes involved in the growth of educational leadership. He further asserted that this concept is a way to think about ethical and effective leadership of principals who diligently work to promote excellence in their schools. This can only be accomplished when such leadership is grounded in meaningful professional practices.

Two groups of researchers discerned four dimensions of authentic leadership – (Brown, Treviño, & Harrison, 2005; Gardner, Avolio, Luthans, May, & Walumbwa, 2005). The four dimensions are as follows:

1. *Self-awareness*: It relates to understanding and creating meaning in the world, and affects the long-term self-perceptions of the leaders. Leaders become

aware of their strong and weak points, and gain awareness concerning the strengths and weaknesses of the people with whom they are in contact. Furthermore, the leaders remain aware of the effect they are having on others.

2. *Balanced processing*: It is the ability to objectively examine and analyze all relevant data before coming to a decision. As a result, leaders who exhibit balanced processing are able to accept opinions that contradict their own.

3. *Relational transparency*: It includes authentic presentation of the self to others. In relational transparency, relationships are built on truth, rather than on presentations of a false selfhood. Trust is created between people, since they are motivated and interested in sharing information with one another and they feel it is important to express genuine thoughts and feelings.

4. *Internalized moral perspective*: It reflects self-regulation, which stems from and is directed by moral standards and autonomous motivation. This is an inner state that emanates from the person, and is not a state dictated by society. When a leader engages in self-regulation, there is synergy between her/his behaviors and her/his internal values.

It is impossible to speak about authentic leadership without relating to professional practice that encompasses the knowledge-base, values, and the process capacities of leaders (Starratt, 2004; Wahlstrom & Louis, 2008). As a result, this aspect helps us better understand the objectives of leadership, and hence makes them more achievable (Begley, 2006).

As discussed above, authentic leadership reflects aspects of the leader's inner self. The leaders, who have a strong sense of who they are and are also sensitive to others, carve out places for themselves in strong corporate and social cultures, since they know how to harness aspects of these cultures for the creations of radical educational–social change (Goffee & Jones, 2005). Many authentic leaders have reported that when they overcome difficult experiences and succeed in solving conflicts, this imbues their leadership with meaning and also leads to significant long-term results (Leroy et al., 2012; Shapira-Lishchinsky & Levy-Gazenfrantz, 2015).

In conclusion, by emphasizing the facets of authentic leadership, educational leaders can gain knowledge and insights into how to deal with ethical dilemmas and engage in ethical decision-making process. As a result, this can empower them in their professional work.

Chapter 12

Ethical Quandaries among Educational Leaders

Hallinger and Heck (2011) argued that educational leaders' missions must have a moral purpose. It is the moral character of a mission that touches people's hearts and engages them. It drives them to act on behalf of something – or someone – beyond their own immediate self-interest. Missions possess motivational forces; they impel us to enter into a shared quest with others in order to accomplish something truly special. This is much more than meeting a productivity goal. Educational leaders often believe that their work is a "calling" filled with meaningful missions and moral challenges.

A school is an ethical organization; every day its leaders face challenges, which call for solving ethical dilemmas and making moral judgments (Shapiro & Stefkovich, 2016). However, when confronted with what has been designated an ethical problem, it is important to ask whether this is what we really are facing. At times, we realize that the case, which was initially perceived to be an ethical problem, is actually right or wrong. In such an instance, what needs to be done will be clear. These kinds of problems differ from ethical quandaries in which other beliefs and ideals lead to different resolutions. When ethical principles come into conflict with one another, we understand that there is no perfect way to act. These are the times in which we must adopt a solution that often falls short of solving the dilemma and, hence, choose a path that does not completely satisfy our principles (Branson & Gross, 2014).

Given this reality, the educational system is in need of leaders who take ethical considerations into account (Marion & Gonzales, 2013). During the course of their day, school principals often confront numerous tasks that connect to ethical questions. For example, school administration needs to deal with problems arising from staff that does not behave according to ethical principles, teachers who abuse students, classes that are far from being homogeneous, parents who are involved in the school but are highly critical of the teachers and the curricula, and school programs, and situations that may occur outside the school, yet deeply impact the school.

Norberg and Johansson (2007) raise a number of dilemmas. For example, should principals focus on concern for the teacher or for the student? What is

International Aspects of Organizational Ethics in Educational Systems, 47–49
Copyright © 2018 by Emerald Publishing Limited
All rights of reproduction in any form reserved
doi:10.1108/978-1-78714-777-520181012

the ethical way to act: to provide more resources for the weak students or for the gifted students? When it comes to issues that divide into majority versus minority opinions, whose side are they on?

Research has been carried out on myriads of ethical problems in leadership (e.g., Eyal, Berkovich, & Schwartz, 2011; Normore, 2011; Shapiro & Stefkovich, 2011). For example, the literature points to a recurring tension between the ethical principle of caring for the other (students and teachers) and the need to follow formal, standard rules (school regulations, professional standards, etc.), which are intended for the good of all. Such situations arise when a principal or other school administrator must decide the optimal way to take care of a student or to respond to peers (Ehrich, Kimber, Millwater, & Cranston, 2011). Take, for example, the case in which an educational leader sees a colleague acting in an unprofessional way, yet feels loyal to this co-worker. This raises the issue of discretion that characterizes relationships between leaders and colleagues (Leithwood & Jantzi, 2005).

The literature further raises another type of difficult ethical quandary that occurs when the school's educational agenda and the student and his/her family do not concur on the educational agenda. This can occur, for example, when a principal is not convinced that parents are acting in the child's best interests (Duignan, 2014).

There are times when education leaders must decide whether they will support parents who propose a different educational agenda from that of the school due to the child's needs (Norberg & Johansson, 2007). Another well-known ethical quandary arises when trying to balance the promotion of egalitarianism while, simultaneously, making sure that students' different needs are met. Strike, Haller, and Soltis (2005) noted that such situations call for school leaders to choose whether or not to favor the principle of fairness and equal allocation of resources, or whether an alternative strategy is needed, the one which allocates resources in differential ways.

Ethical quandaries also often appear when stakeholders attempt to assert their autonomy in order to meet objectives they see as important in the school. These may be individuals working in the school (teachers, students, and administration) or people from the community (parents and local authorities). As could be expected, different interested parties can also hold different ideas about what is "good," leading to questions of whose viewpoint should be accepted (Baete, 2011). In this case, educational leaders may find themselves forced to make decisions against their own conscience. Such decisions are not made lightly; they often have moral consequences. Unfortunately, this is not a rare occurrence; educational leaders must often deal with multiple, and sometimes contradictory, demands by different people inside and outside the school (Starratt, 2004).

Fig. 12.1 maps the main tensions that are inherent to ethical quandaries discussed above among educational leaders: Caring for others (teachers and students) vs complying with formal school rules; concern for the teacher vs caring for the students; following one's conscience vs adopting contradictory demands of stakeholders; promoting students egalitarianism vs attending to differential needs; school's educational agenda vs family's educational agenda; supporting teachers' autonomy vs. school interests; and finally, showing discretion (of students or teachers) versus emphasizing relationships with colleagues.

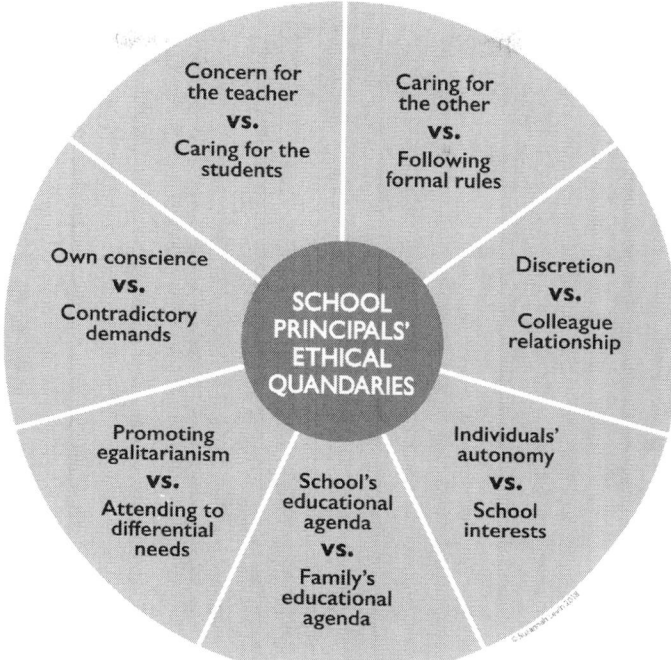

Fig. 12.1:   School Principals' Ethical Quandaries (© Susannah Levin 2018).

It seems that awareness to the school principals' ethical quandaries may promote ethical decision making among educational leaders. The following chapter will discuss this subject.

Chapter 13

Ethical Decision Making among Educational Leaders

According to Kohls and Christensen (2002), an ethical decision-making process occurs when the person or authoritative body making the decision has taken into account the core values and interests of all stakeholders. Ethical decision making in organizations can only be accomplished if we understand the importance of the interaction between individual and situational components. Deciding on whether a particular stance or behavior is ethical or not (right or wrong) is dependent upon the cognitive-moral development stage of the person. Nevertheless, knowledge of right and wrong on its own cannot fully explain or predict ethical decision-making behavior. There are other situational factors which need to be taken into account. These include the job's framework, ethical content of the organizational culture, and the importance of obeying authority and rules. When these factors interact with the individual's cognitive understanding and development, this significantly impacts how one responds to an ethical dilemma (Treviño, Weaver, & Reynolds, 2006).

While managers and administrators in all fields of work often need to make decisions that have ethical implications, they have not always received adequate knowledge of *how* to properly respond to a situation. Given the essence of the educational field, it is paramount that educational leaders know how to deal with ethical dilemmas, for at least two reasons. To begin with, they dedicate their work lives to people (as opposed to products), and second, given their training and knowledge, teachers, students, and parents often seek them out for advice on how to successfully meet ethical challenges that arise (Mills, 2006).

School principals are often called upon to reach ethical decisions in team environments. For example, at school board meetings, they work on budgets and come to decisions concerning how to divide resources; they design curricula in meetings with curriculum coordinators; and they confer with parents in parent committees and on the school board. Many of these joint activities raise ethical issues, and principals are called upon to explain how they reached certain decisions. Among others, they need to assure the stakeholders that decisions were made in a fair manner; that decisions concerning how to distribute resources sought just and equitable solutions; that the teachers, under their auspices, acted

International Aspects of Organizational Ethics in Educational Systems, 51–52
Copyright © 2018 by Emerald Publishing Limited
All rights of reproduction in any form reserved
doi:10.1108/978-1-78714-777-520181013

in fair and humane ways; and that the students who were disciplined were sanctioned in fitting and just ways.

As a result, it is clear that ethical decision making in a team is an essential part of the school principal's functions. His/her work is inherently tied to the issues of fairness, equality, justice, and democracy. While we may think that school principals are mainly concerned with how well their students perform at standard tests, teachers' promotions, parents, and allocation of limited resources, the ethical parts of their job are no less important (Strike, Haller, & Soltis, 2005).

Section III

Cross-National Aspects of the Relationship Between Perceptions of Organizational Ethics and Teachers' Withdrawal Behaviors

Chapter 14

Organizational Ethics in Educational Systems

This chapter addresses a number of facets of organizational ethical perceptions (distributive justice, procedural justice, caring climate, formal climate, and ethical culture). Here, these constructs were selected for discussion for two reasons: in recent years, there have been many studies on these topics, and because their exploration makes it possible to predict teachers' behaviors such as withdrawal behaviors and organizational citizenship behaviors.

Swift changes occurring in educational systems raise many ethical questions, which, in turn, affect organizational ethics (Ingersoll & May, 2012; Ingersoll, Merrill, & May, 2016). When addressing organizational ethics in educational systems, a focus is placed on values held by school leaders, ones they expect their teachers to embrace and ones that will most likely characterize the school environment. As a result, this influences the perceptions that teachers have of internal and external stimuli and the way they respond to such stimuli (Shapira-Lishchinsky & Rosenblatt, 2010).

Organizational Justice

It ishighly important to study the concept of organizational justice if we want to understand interpersonal relationships and organizational processes. Furthermore, it is deeply rooted in the equity theory (Adams, 1965; Greenberg & Cohen, 2014). Organizational justice describes the role of fairness in the workplace (Greenberg & Colquitt, 2013). It centers on the processes by which individuals determine whether they have been treated fairly or not, and it looks at the ways in which these perceptions affect other consequences. Research that has been carried out on organizational justice has continually demonstrated that workers expect organizational decisions to be fair. As a result, when employees feel that decisions are *not* made in a just or fair manner, they tend to react negatively to their workplace (Moorman & Byrne, 2013; Rupp, Shapiro, Folger, Skarlicki, & Shao, 2017).

Research has focused on two main categories of justice: distributive justice and procedural justice. *Procedural justice* describes the fairness of the procedures used to determine organizational outcomes (Pillai, Williams, & Justin Tan, 2001). In the school context, fairness can be expressed, for example, through transparency

International Aspects of Organizational Ethics in Educational Systems, 55–60
Copyright © 2018 by Emerald Publishing Limited
All rights of reproduction in any form reserved
doi:10.1108/978-1-78714-777-520181014

concerning how school principals are chosen for their positions or if teachers can appeal a decision made by the school's administration that they feel is wrong. Another example is when teachers feel that the school principal has carefully explained how and why s/he reached a certain decision (Loerbroks et al., 2014).

Distributive justice refers to the fair-mindedness of the results employees receive in relation to the work they have carried out in the organization (Greenberg & Colquitt, 2005). Distributive justice, in the context of the school, focuses on the perception of the justice, which is a result of the school's decisions concerning the division of roles, rewards, and consideration of the personal needs of the teachers. These include issues such as the level of monetary rewards for different jobs, for example, of being in charge of pedagogical matters, constructing the teaching schedule, and carrying a heavy work load. According to this kind of justice, a teacher may evaluate the results that s/he received in comparison to certain standards of justice (Altinkurt, Yilmaz, & Karaman, 2015). As a result, for example, the teacher may decide if her/his monthly salary fits her/his level of investment in the school. Does it adequately reflect the number of hours that s/he works both in the school and outside the building when undertaking school-related activities? This examination can be undertaken in comparison to what workers get in the public sector.

Although both distributive and procedural justices reflect teachers' perception of justice in their respective organizations, the two concepts are distinctly different. Resh and Sabbagh (2014) argue that while sense of distributive justice can be perceived as the individual's evaluation of the gap between actual and deserved reward, procedural justice can be perceived as an institutional (school) feature. Thus, according to their approach, perception of procedural justice develops over time, while perception of distributive justice may be local and momentary.

The academic literature notes two main impacts on the perception of organizational justice. On the one hand, there is the perception of justice and its appropriateness in terms of the social and cultural context that shapes it (James, 2015). On the other hand, organizational justice can also be viewed as an outgrowth of the organization itself. Over time, people working in the same organizational unit develop a similar kind of evaluation of justice due to their common experiences. For example, they will evaluate the justice concerning how rewards are divided (Colquitt, LePine, Piccolo, Zapata, & Rich, 2012). We also see that in order to understand the concept of justice in schools, there is a need to consider the social value system that exists outside the classroom or school, for example, the system in the community and the value system that develops within the school itself.

Ethical Climate

For the last 20 years, there has been much research on the ethical climate in the school. The researchers who established the basis for this field of inquiry are Victor and Cullen (1988) and Cullen, Parboteeah, and Victor (2003). The researchers provided a definition of ethical climate, noting that it reflects employees' perceptions of organizational norms regarding behaviors and decisions, including those acts and decisions that involve ethical content. The ethical climate provides a perceptual lens for employees, turning them into observers, which makes it possible for them to evaluate situations. This facilitates their identification of ethical issues, necessary when attempting to solve problems (Cullen, Victor, & Bronson, 1993).

Victor and Cullen (1988) conceptualized the ethical climate as comprised two dimensions: (a) the basic ethical elements of *egoism* (the motivation to maximize fulfillment of one's self-interests), *benevolence* (the motivation to attain maximum joint interests), and *principle* (fulfillment of moral values). The second dimension consists of three levels of analysis: the *individual, local* (organizational), and *cosmopolitan* (societal).

Cross-tabulation of the two factors yields nine ethical climates, which Victor and Cullen (1988) collapsed into five ethical climates: (a) *caring* (egoism at the cosmopolitan level and benevolence at all levels. In this climate, employees, deeply care about the welfare of others, whether or not they are part of the organization); (b) *instrumental* (this reflects egoism on the individual and local levels. The most important interests are perceived as being individual and organizational ones); (c) *rules* (this reflects principles connected to the local level; employees tend to follow organizational regulations and procedures); (d) *law and code* (this ethical climate reflects adhering to principles on the cosmopolitan level. In this case, employees are guided by laws, regulations, and professional codes); and (e) *independence* (principle on the individual level; employees are guided by personal beliefs and morality).

Since publication of this research on ethical climates in organizations, other researchers have also adopted this five-factor structure (e.g., Weber, 1995). When Rosenblatt and Peled (2002) undertook a study that replicated the five-dimension solution of ethical school climate, they found the climates determined to be caring and formal were the two most powerful and valid predictors of school outcomes. Since a caring school climate expresses concern for everyone impacted by decisions made at the school, promotes compassion, and stresses the need to pay attention to personal and social needs, we can easily understand why teachers would cherish such an ethical climate, given that it meets their needs and interests as well.

The formal climate – a combination of the two categories of rules and law and codes (Victor and Cullen, 1988) – reflects a climate in which school leaders expect employees to follow the organization's rules and to abide by their profession's codes and regulations. Through ethical rules, people who are connected to the school learn acceptable behaviors, come to know which values are the ideals that are highly regarded in the organization, and what actions they need to take in order to be rewarded (Appelbaum, Iaconi, & Matousek, 2007). Therefore, it follows that teachers will appreciate a formal climate, since such a climate provides a protective shield from abusive organizational processes.

Ethical Culture

"Organizational culture," which reflects the values, beliefs, and assumptions that are shared by people in an organization (Schein, 2010), is a type of informal control system that comprises common traditions (Ruiz-Palomino & Martínez-Cañas, 2014). The specific ethical culture of an organization refers to the experiences, assumptions, and expectations of an organization concerning how it encourages its members to conduct themselves ethically (Ruiz-Palomino, Martínez-Cañas, & Fontrodona, 2013; Trevino & Weaver, 2003). Therefore, ethical culture can be defined as the facets of the perceived organizational context that have the potential to encourage its members to act in an ethical manner while minimizing unethical behavior. As seen in previous research (e.g., Kish-Gephart, Harrison, & Treviño, 2010), the ethical culture mirrors how the organization actually engages in its practice in terms of what constitutes ethical and unethical behavior.

Kaptein (2008a), who continued this line of research, expanded the construct of ethical culture by adding numerous normative dimensions. His focus, which was on the virtues of the normative dimensions, denoted the following:

1. *Clarity of ethical standards*: To what degree employees and leaders are expected to follow the ethical standards that have been determined?
2. *Ethical role modeling of management and supervisors*: Do the leaders serve as good role models for their staff in terms of ethical behavior? If so, to what degree? According to the social learning theory (Bandura, 1977), individuals often learn how they are supposed to behave by modeling the behaviors of others in authority, after carefully observing them.
3. *Feasibility*: This dimension reflects the conditions that organizations generate that can help employees act according to normative expectations. As Kaptein (2011) noted, unethical conduct tends to occur in situations in which workers do not have the time, budget, equipment, information, and authority they need to do their jobs in a satisfactory manner. Treviño and Youngblood's (1990) explanation of these results argued that people who constantly work under conditions of pressure tend to take less note of others' legitimate expectations from them in comparison to individuals who do have adequate time or resources.
4. *Supportability*: This aspect examines the support the organization is providing for administrators' and workers' ethical conduct. In other words, supportability addresses the degree to which a person identifies with, is involved in, and expresses commitment to her/his organization's normative expectations. It further asks how much the organization stimulates ethical behavior.
5. *Transparency (visibility)*: Transparency looks at the extent to which people in the organization are afforded true opportunities to see the consequences of (un)ethical behavior on the part of leaders and employees. Transparency comprises two elements: (a) a vertical component that reflects the extent to which leaders can observe unethical conduct and its consequences of employees (top-down) and vice versa (bottom-up); and (b) a horizontal component that reflects the degree to which employees can observe unethical conduct and its consequences among themselves.
6. *Discussability*: Another important dimension reflects employees' and leaders' opportunities to enter into dialogues concerning different ethical issues, such

as ethical dilemmas or alleged unethical behaviors. Edwards and Shepherd (2007) noted that the communication theory has demonstrated that when people talk about important issues that concern them, they not only learn from one another, but also reach higher levels of respect for one another, due to these dialogues. In fact, when an organizational culture consistently encourages silencing of talk about moral issues, an amoral organizational culture often develops. This is because by avoiding honest discussion of moral issues, they go unnoticed. This ultimately leads to two phenomena: a higher level of moral stress and a decrease in the moral authority of ethical standard.

7. *Sanctionability*. It reflects the extent of enforcement of ethical behavior. This is accomplished through punishment when a person acts in an unethical manner, and through rewards to people who behave in ethically sound ways. The reinforcement theory (Collins, Jackson, Walker, O'Connor, & Gardiner, 2017) posits that the consequences of a decision made in the past influence decision-making in the future. As a result, a person rewarded for his/her ethical behavior will tend to repeat such behavior, whereas a punishment for unethical behavior should influence an individual to avoid such behavior.

Kaptein (2008a) fashioned these dimensions into a Corporate Ethical Virtues (CEV) model and created a self-reported questionnaire that measures the ethical culture of organizations. The CEV model was tested and validated in a number of places in the world among managers, employees and university students. These included the countries of: the United States (Kaptein, 2010), the Democratic Republic of Congo (DRC) (Mitonga-Monga & Cilliers, 2015), Malaysia (Sami, Jusoh, Mahfar, Qureshi, & Khan, 2016); the Netherlands (Kaptein, 2011), and Finland and Lithuania (Riivari & Lämsä, 2014).

Based on research that took into account the stakeholders' perspectives and the use of business codes of ethics, Kaptein (2008b) developed the meaning of ethical culture. Furthermore, by presenting and analyzing cases from the field that involved different kinds of unethical employee conduct that were caused by the organizational culture, Kaptein's 2004 study was actually the first research project that collected and analyzed the business codes of multinational companies. His large, multinational research, which explored 105 companies that had a business code of ethics in 11 different countries (the United States, France, Germany, Japan, Switzerland, England, Italy, the Netherlands, South Korea, Canada, and Sweden) created a common meaning for the concept of ethical culture.

These studies, which explored business and public organizations, with the goal of gaining core knowledge and validation of the meanings and dimensions of ethical culture, have become central in the study of ethics in organizations. However, to date, no study has investigated the concept of ethical culture in educational systems. If we use Kaptein's (2011) conceptualizations as a basis for the educational context, we can propose that ethical culture in schools may be viewed as a result of the interplay between the formal (e.g., educational policy, teachers' codes of ethics) and informal (e.g., norms concerning school ethics) aspects that can augment ethical behavior among educators. It is hoped that the future research will use this concept in exploring ethics in educational systems.

Confusion Around the Definitions of Culture and Climate in the Context of Ethics

Previous studies have posited different ideas concerning how the concepts of culture and climate should be defined and delineated from each other. For example, Schein (2010) considered climate as an artifact of culture, defining culture as shared norms, values, and assumptions, while Denison (1996) saw culture and climate as not really being different from each other. Other past research, however, averred that ethical culture and ethical climate are two distinct phenomena. For example, Kaptein (2011) distinguished between ethical culture and ethical climate, considering ethical culture as responsible for the actual conditions for ethical behaviors, while perceiving the ethical climate as reflective of stakeholders' understandings about what constitutes ethical behavior in their organizations.

In a similar vein, Trevino Butterfield, and McCabe (1998) found a strong positive correlation between ethical culture and climate. Nevertheless, these researchers argue that the two concepts are not the same. Ethical climate relates to attitudes, while ethical culture relates more to impacts on actions. As a result, ethical culture may explain unethical behavior in a better way than ethical climate. Therefore, considering the fact that many studies have addressed the ethical climate in the school, while none has explored ethical culture in schools, this book has embarked on this much-needed concept.

Relations Between the Dimensions of Organizational Ethics

Each of the ethical concepts noted above represents a different facet of organizational ethics and are closely related to one another. For example, over 35 years ago, Gilligan (1982) argued that the ethics of care and justice are interrelated, since they both revolve around responsibility and social relationships. In addition, both care and justice consider morality as the way to solve conflicts between people. The concepts of the formal climate and distributive justice are also closely related to one another because both address workers' rights and an organization's rules and regulations that are necessary for ensuring that benefits are divided in a fair manner between employees.

At times, tension can arise between some of the values that are reflective of the ethical concepts, such as caring and equality-based distributive justice. A model conceptualized by Cameron and Quinn (2011), entitled the *competing values model*, avers that this conflict can actually contribute to organizational effectiveness. This is because when people engage in a dialogue, which brings to the fore opposing positions, the values can come to be seen as being complementary instead of conflicting. Therefore, this has the potential to enable incorporation of opposing positions (Colnerud, 2006; Shapiro & Stefkovich, 2010), which may, in the end, provide a broadened perspective when dealing with teachers' behaviors.

Chapter 15

Teachers' Withdrawal Behaviors

My previous studies indicated that perceptions of organizational ethics in schools predict teachers' withdrawal behaviors (e.g., Shapira-Lishchinsky, 2007, 2009a, 2011); therefore, the following chapters focus on these behaviors among teachers. Withdrawal behaviors refer to perceptions, attitudes, and behaviors of employees who remain in their positions but for some reason participate to a lesser degree than they used to do in their organizations (Camden, Price, & Ludwig, 2011; Kaplan, Bradley, Luchman, & Haynes, 2009). Defining work by time is critical because time is a scarce organizational and individual resource and can be easily used or abused (Nätti, Oinas, Härmä, Anttila, & Kandolin, 2014).

Comparative studies maintain that context is a powerful factor of withdrawal behaviors. For example, Addae, Johns, and Boies (2013) showed that legitimacy of absences varies in different cultures, both between and within societies. It is likely that the social culture shapes the educational policy context, and educational policy in turn, impacts teachers' behaviors.

Examples of withdrawal behaviors include tardiness, absenteeism, turnover, and attrition. The reason why it is so important to research on such behaviors among teachers and educators is because teachers' withdrawal behaviors turn out to be very costly for the school and negatively impacts school standards and ethics. Moreover, such behaviors also increase pressure on the other employees. This results in lower levels of morale in the schools (McInerney, Ganotice, King, Marsh, & Morin, 2015; Shapira-Lishchinsky & Tsemach, 2014).

Relationships between Different Withdrawal Behaviors

Researchers (e.g., Koslowsky, Sagie, Krausz, & Singer, 1997; Miraglia & Johns, 2016) have proposed that there are four main theoretical models that describe the relationships that exist between different withdrawal behaviors. These include the following: the independent model, the spillover model, the compensatory model, and the progression model.

International Aspects of Organizational Ethics in Educational Systems, 61–67
Copyright © 2018 by Emerald Publishing Limited
All rights of reproduction in any form reserved
doi:10.1108/978-1-78714-777-520181015

- Joy (2016) asserted that in an independent model, withdrawal behaviors have different causes and functions. As a result, they are unrelated to one another. According to this model, workers can choose different methods of withdrawal.
- The spillover model asserts that withdrawal behaviors are positively related to one another, but it does not outline temporal or sequential relationships (Wood & Michaelides, 2016). Therefore, according to this model, it is quite probable that a person will react to certain conditions with a number of withdrawal behaviors, and not with just one withdrawal behavior.
- The compensatory model offers another explanation: It asserts that similar functionality will lead to particular forms of withdrawal that are negatively correlated with one another (Harrison, Newman, & Roth, 2006).
- The progressive model is the most common model. This model avers that withdrawal behaviors move along a continuum. They begin with fairly mild forms of psychological withdrawal, for example, tardiness every now and then. They then progress to more severe forms, with employees taking absences and deciding to turnover or attrite (Sagie, Birati, & Tziner, 2002).

To sum up, studies have not yet proposed one clear single model that can explain how the various withdrawal behaviors relate to one another. In fact, the results are ambiguous to a certain extent. There have been some scholars who have asserted that the behaviors are unrelated to one another (e.g., Staw & Ross, 1987); others have reported negative relationships (Nicholson & Goodge, 1976); some researchers found positive relationships (Iverson & Deery, 2001; Leigh & Lust, 1988), while others have reported that no sequential relationship between the behaviors have been found and that they actually take place simultaneously (Benson & Pond, 1987; Wolpin & Burke, 1985).

These varied and contradictory findings led me to address the differences between the dimensions of teachers' withdrawal behaviors, such as tardiness, absenteeism, turnover, and attrition, by exploring them through ethical predictors. This approach could not only create some order in the muddy results but could also help decrease such negative behaviors on the part of teachers (Rosenblatt & Shapira-Lishchinsky, 2017).

Teachers' Tardiness

Tardiness is described as arriving late at work or leaving before the workday is over (Koslowsky, 2000). Since schools operate on a time table that is quite rigid, it also refers to a teacher's lack of arriving on time to her/his classes. People can be late for many reasons, and the reasons often depend on their cultural norms. For example, it has been proposed that when people from developing countries arrive late to class, they may actually be acting appropriately according to their culture, which has a flexible conceptualization of time, but differs significantly from the concept of time characteristic of developed countries (White, Valk, & Dialmy, 2011). Thus, tardiness could certainly reflect a cultural context and not reflect how the person relates to her/his organization. However, this is not the case in developed countries: there lateness usually reflects job withdrawal (Foust, Elicker, & Levy, 2006).

If we adopt the progression theory of employee withdrawal (Koslowsky et al., 1997), tardiness is perceived as a "less severe" form of withdrawal. Over time, it can escalate into worse forms of absenteeism and attrition. There have been numerous research attempts to understand and increase productivity; one area that has been studied in depth is how to decrease withdrawal behaviors, since they often disturb work schedules and harm productivity (Edralin, 2015).

Tardiness has "motivational" antecedents and can be classified as having three dimensions: chronic, unavoidable, and avoidable.

- *Chronic tardiness* reflects employees' dislike of a very unpleasant work situation. Relevant antecedents to chronic tardiness include commitment to the organization and job satisfaction.
- *Unavoidable tardiness* is caused by reasons beyond the worker's control. These include factors such as problems getting to and from school, inclement weather, sickness, and accidents (Blau, 2002).
- Employees will engage in *avoidable tardiness* (stable periodic tardiness) when they feel that they have better or more important things to do than arrive on time. Antecedents to this kind of tardiness can include leisure–income tradeoff or a work–family conflict (Balow, 2015).

In short, tardiness can be a result of unavoidable situations, but can also derive from avoidable factors that are based in perceived unethical conditions. One example is when teachers make the decision not to come to school on time because they feel that their free time takes precedence over their job responsibilities, or because they dislike their work.

Teachers' Absenteeism

Absenteeism is defined as the lack of physical presence at a behavioral setting, when and where one is expected to be (Allisey, Rodwell, & Noblet, 2016). There is no doubt that employees' absences are a major human resource management problem. The financial costs of absenteeism are a direct result of having to replace workers and the diminished productivity that results from employees' absences. Moreover, when teachers miss work, this negatively impacts the quality of education the students are receiving: both achievement levels and student attendance levels have been found to suffer (Duflo, Hanna, & Ryan, 2012). In addition, we must add indirect costs, such as complications involved in replacing highly skilled employees providing necessary services with personnel who may not have similar training and experience. This then often leads to less than acceptable performances (Ybema, van der Meer, & Leijten, 2016).

The relative lack of research on the consequences of teacher absenteeism is regrettable, since their absence negatively impacts their students. In studies that have been carried out, it has been found that such behavior reduces student motivation to attend school and thus may in turn increase student absenteeism (Apple, Au, & Gandin, 2011). Furthermore, when student's learning is interrupted, this can contribute to lower levels of academic achievement (Ejere, 2010; Miller,

Murnane, & Willett, 2008). Research has also found that teachers often resort to absenteeism due to simultaneous and connected problems, such as their resistance to change or input, their increase in negative feelings, and decreased levels of motivations to come to work (Derycke, Vlerick, Van de Ven, Rots, & Clays, 2013).

There are numerous reasons why teachers might miss class. A teacher may be sick and, therefore, unable to work; they may not be able to make it to class since they have a conflicting commitment that cannot be rescheduled (e.g., a long-awaited and important doctor's appointment); the teacher prefers to be somewhere else; and/or the teacher decides to take a paid 'vacation' day, when s/he is not suffering from a health problem that requires rest or treatment (Shapira-Lishchinsky & Raftar-Ozery, 2016). These reasons can be sorted into two general approaches concerning the person's decision to be absent – reasons under the teacher's control (voluntary), and those not under their control (involuntary) (Carlsen, 2012).

Whatever the reasons, many studies (e.g., Deery, Walsh, & Zatzick, 2014) have looked for relationships between work absence and perceptions of work, and tended to show that absence is predicted by the following: job satisfaction and commitment to one's work place (Harrison & Martocchio, 1998); workers' perceptions of the social context characteristics of their employment (Martocchio & Jimeno, 2003); and employees' perceptions of their manager's leadership style in terms of how supportive it is (Hassan, Wright, & Yukl, 2014).

The academic literature on organizational behavior, especially the literature that emphasizes educational organizations, has shown that absenteeism clearly relates to job perceptions and attitudes, such as organizational justice and organizational commitment (Hassard, Teoh, & Cox, 2016; Khan, Nawaz, Qureshi, & Khan, 2016). These research projects demonstrated that teachers who hold negative attitudes about their schools tend to miss work.

Voluntary versus Involuntary Measures of Absence

Over time, the academic literature on absenteeism has highlighted that *voluntary* and *involuntary* measures of absence need to be differentiated from one another (Johns & Al Hajj, 2015; Sagie, 1998; Shantz & Alfes, 2015). Furthermore, this typology has focused on the voluntary control of absence. The researchers differentiated between these categories because through this categorization they were able to explain more of the criterion variance (Johns, 1997); it produced "purified" measures, and as a result was able to improve predictability and stability (Xie & Johns, 2000).

- *Voluntary absence* refers to missing work for reasons that the employees can control, such as taking time off for pastime activities or to search for new employment. Management generally works very hard at containing and reducing such work absences. As a rule of thumb, voluntary absence is measured by its frequency; for example, the number of times the employee misses work. Thus, in this case, the length of each absence event is not calculated. Academics who study this issue agree that episodic absence is a good signifier of the worker's negative perceptions of work. An employee who has a high score on absence frequency will often miss work, although these absences will be short (that is, "skip days"). These frequent absences are indications that the worker does not wish to come into work (Shapira-Lishchinsky & Even-Zohar, 2011).

- *Involuntary absence* is missing work for reasons that the employee cannot control, such as illness or important family events that the worker cannot miss (mourning, marriage, etc.). This kind of absence is typically measured by the time lost: an absence spell of 20 days is calculated higher than an absence that lasted for two days; with the frequency measure, each of these two is scored equally as one absence episode (Shapira-Lishchinsky, 2012).

It is generally believed that absenteeism frequency is the best way to distinguish between voluntary absenteeism and involuntary absenteeism (Blau, Surges Tatum, & Ward Cook, 2004; Sagie, 1998). For instance, two teachers miss work for 10 days during a school year. In the first case, the teacher misses 10 days in a row for one event. In the second case, the teacher misses 10 days, but is gone for two days at a time for five different occasions. Here, we would reach the conclusion that the first teacher was gone due to involuntary reasons, since it seems very unlikely that a teacher would choose to miss work for 10 consecutive days at one event. Therefore, if a teacher misses so many work days for one reason, there must be a strong reason that s/he did not come to work it may be due to an involuntary reason (e.g., a tragedy occurred in the teacher's family and she was in mourning). However, it would appear to us that the second teacher was gone for five times, two days each time, because he/she deliberately and voluntarily made the choice to miss school for a number of short periods.

Whether these assumptions concerning the above scenarios reflect the reality or not, research that has been carried out on educational systems (e.g., Shapira-Lishchinsky & Rosenblatt, 2009a, 2009b) demonstrates that it is not always easy to come to a definitive answer if an absence should be classified as voluntary or involuntary. For example, what is the most appropriate way to classify absences of a teacher who missed school to look for new employment after learning that he would not be rehired for the next year? Is it a voluntary absence because he chose to be absent to look for another job (e.g., interviews in other schools), or is it an involuntary absence, since he knew that he would not be rehired for the next year, and therefore he must be absent from his school to look for another job?

Therefore, although we assume that attitudes can impact measures of voluntary absenteeism (absence frequency) more than they affect absence duration, it appears that it is best to study both absenteeism frequency and absenteeism duration. In our study (Shapira-Lishchinsky & Ishan, 2013), we obtained a relatively high correlation between absence frequency and absence duration ($r = 0.714$, $p < 0.001$), which lent support for this methodological approach.

In order to present a more complex picture, it is important to note that there have been some studies (Hackett & Bycio, 1996; Staw & Oldham, 1978) that have demonstrated that tardiness and absenteeism are not solely detrimental to organizations. These researchers have asserted that these behaviors can give employees a needed break from job dissatisfaction and stress. Furthermore, tardiness and absenteeism could even be expected if the workers face numerous injurious aspects at their place of employment. As a result, if teachers come in late or are absent a bit, they may later return to work with higher levels of motivation. This could, in turn, increase organizational effectiveness, in the long run. However, in order to paint a realistic picture, it cannot be overlooked that the majority of studies (e.g., Rosenblatt & Shapira-Lishchinsky, 2017; Sagie, Elizur, & Koslowsky, 1996) understand withdrawal behaviors to be a manifestation of unethical behaviors and the results of negative perceptions regarding school ethics.

Teacher Turnover and Attrition

In the educational systems, when researchers study teacher turnover, they are referring to internal mobility versus external mobility. When teachers move from one school to another, or when they move to higher or lower positions, they remain in the educational system. This is different than teachers' attrition, teachers who leave the profession, for reasons unconnected to retirement (Richardson & Watt, 2016). In recent years, there has been an increase of teachers' attrition, reflected by leaving the profession. Studies that focus on the rate of attrition note that it is especially high among young teachers in their first five years of employment (Delp, 2014; Goldhaber & Cowan, 2014; Ronfeldt, Loeb, & Wyckoff, 2013). When numerous researchers across countries describe the present situation, they express fear about the growing trend of teacher attrition in the western world. The strongest tendency is among young teachers who decide to leave the profession forever (Clandinin et al., 2015; Global Education Monitoring Report, 2016; Hansen, Backes, & Brady, 2016).

The academic discussion around the reasons that teachers leave the teaching profession relates to three main categories: *personal reasons*, such as age, burnout, difficulties in dealing with stress (Ju, Lan, Li, Feng, & You, 2015; Wang, Hall, & Rahimi, 2015); *organizational reasons*, such as organizational culture, employment requirements, pay, cooperation with colleagues, and discipline of students (Berg & Cornell, 2016; Long et al., 2012); and *external reasons* that are derived from the fact that the teaching profession is not perceived as being an attractive and prestigious profession in school communities and in many countries throughout the world (Shapira-Lishchinsky, 2009b). Furthermore, the level of teachers' pay, even with all of the changes that have taken place in the educational systems in the world, is still perceived in most societies as being low to average. In addition, there are relatively few opportunities for advancement (Ingersoll & May, 2012; Ingersoll, Merrill, & Stuckey, 2014). This is because the educational system is perceived as being a flat system (Litchka & Shapira-Lishchinsky, 2016).

Studies have shown that when many quality teachers leave the profession, this may harm the educational process, student achievement, school stability, negatively impact the commitment of other teachers and the ability of the principal to mainatian a smooth running of school (Jacob, Goddard, Kim, Miller, & Goddard, 2015; Kaimal & Jordan, 2016). In addition, one of the central problems related to teacher attrition is that schools then need to recruit new teachers to replace the ones who left. As a result, it takes quite a bit of time for the new teachers to gain experience and to learn how the school works. These processes take time and require financial and human resources (Ingersoll, Merrill, & May, 2016).

Nevertheless, in the modern employment world, moving between jobs and employment changes are not out of the ordinary, and the teaching profession is no different than other professions, in this matter. Therefore, we should not necessarily expect that the teaching profession will be one in which every teacher remains for her/his entire life. Moreover, a low rate of teacher attrition is not necessarily a positive thing, since it keeps new energies and ideas from being introduced into schools and into the teaching profession (Shapira-Lishchinsky & Rosenblatt, 2009b). Therefore, in the framework of this discussion about teacher attrition, it is important to examine which teachers decide to leave, which ones decide to stay, and what are the factors that contribute to these decisions.

Chapter 16

Ethical Aspects of Teachers' Withdrawal Behaviors

Research done during the last few years (Carpenter & Berry, 2017; Koslowsky, 2009; Zimmerman, Swider, Woo, & Allen, 2016) have found that withdrawal behaviors may be the result of attitudes and perceptions that could have been avoided – that is from employees perceiving that their organization allowed unethical conditions to prevail, a phenomenon which reduced organizational effectiveness. Workers who hold such perceptions, attitudes, and behaviors are likely to reduce their energy at work, in direct or indirect ways, and this may be a sign that the organization is characterized by at least some degree of unethical behaviors (Burke, Tomlinson, & Cooper, 2016). These results demonstrate how important it is to explore the ethical predictors that can lead to solid predictions concerning withdrawal behaviors among teachers.

Research has found that withdrawal behaviors are often under the employee's control. In other words, withdrawal behaviors are usually voluntary. Therefore, it is often the case that the perspective of the employee concerning ethics can explain why he/she choose to withdraw from work (Shapira-Lishchinsky & Tsemach, 2014). When studying such behaviors in the context of schools, it has been found that tardiness and absence adversely affect students, who are entitled to a proper education (Bowers, 2001). As a rule, there is no compensation for the time that is lost when a teacher is late for class. However, this is not usually the case for absences (for example, when the teacher notifies the administration that s/he will not be able to make it to school at the last minute). These absences tend to be made up by colleagues who have their own responsibilities, thus adding to their workload (Bowers & McIver, 2000).

Considering the withdrawal behaviors of turnover and attrition, teachers who decide to leave and move to other positions, take the knowledge, experience, and skills they have acquired at their educational positions and are able to transfer them to the organizations where they find new employment. This reduces the morale of their former colleagues (Ingersoll, Merrill, & May, 2016).

International Aspects of Organizational Ethics in Educational Systems, 69–71
Copyright © 2018 by Emerald Publishing Limited
doi:10.1108/978-1-78714-777-520181016

In sum, the motivation for engaging in withdrawal behaviors may be due to different personal and work-related reasons. However, all of the voluntary behaviors may share the elements of potentially unethical behavior.

Ethical Aspects of Teachers' Tardiness

Tardiness differs from absences because tardiness can be hidden, at least partially, as opposed to absences, which is much more difficult to conceal. For example, a teacher can come late to class without the tardiness being recorded. Perhaps, for this reason, absences are almost always recorded by the human resources department in educational systems, as opposed to tardiness, which is not recorded in places that do not have a system, such as a punch clock, for documenting when a teacher arrives at school. Furthermore, lateness will not be recorded during the day when there is no surveillance process put into place in the classrooms (Shapira-Lishinsky, 2012). As a result, today, in many countries, there is no enforcement measure that can prevent teachers from coming late to school, sometimes due to resistance on the part of teachers organizations. This further means that there is no tracking of costs of lateness from either an economic or learning aspect.

When a teacher arrives late for his/her work day, or when a teacher comes late to class for reasons unconnected to the need to provide emergency treatment for students' problems, an educational ethical condition arises because the teacher increases his/her leisure time on account of his/her teaching, for which s/he receives monetary compensation. An additional ethical problem is that tardiness can be good for the tardy person while harming others. For example, a teacher who is late for class, because she is running personal errands, may cause discipline problems for her students, place a burden on the administration and the other teachers, since the administration and other teachers will have to deal with these disciplinary problems until she shows up, and harms making progress on the material. The ethical problem worsens with the teacher's response concerning their tardiness. When they are asked to explain why they were late, they have a tendency to downplay the harm their tardinesscaused (Rosenblatt & Shapira-Lishchinsky, 2017).

Ethical Aspects of Teachers' Absences

When two contradictory cognitions exist simultaneously – "it is unethical to miss class," on the one hand, and "I am taking an absence," on the other – the teachers develop cognitive dissonance. In order to avoid feeling this dissonance, teachers tend to relate their absences to the factors beyond their control, factors that justify missing the class, such as being sick, and not to the factors they can control, such as the desire to run errands instead of taking class, a job to which they committed (Shapira-Lischinsky, 2012).

Teachers are not the only persons who often take absences; this is a widespread phenomenon of public sector. Previous studies (e.g., Mowday, Porter, & Steers, 2013) point out that there is an illogical relationship between a physician's diagnosis and the number of sick leaves taken by a worker. According to the researchers, doctors often issue official letters that a worker was ill, due to pressure brought to bear by employees who do not want to go to work. It appears as if employees, at times, think that work absence is their right. As a result, they use it as a way to protest things that they do not accept about their workplace.

Another ethical problem arises in relation to the economic loss that results from false reporting of voluntary absences. For example, teachers receive payment for "sick days" for unjustified absences when in fact they could have come to school. This is in addition to the ethical problems that arise due to their absence. For example, there is an abuse of the resource of time of the school's administration, that is, when a teacher is absent, the administration needs to allocate time for finding a suitable solution to the teacher's absence, such as bringing in a substitute teacher, and for treating disciplinary problems in the classroom of the absent teacher. This comes at the expense of allocating time for work that could facilitate the school's progress (Rosenblatt & Shapira-Lishchinsky, 2017).

Moreover, studies on calendric absence trends (e.g., Alcázar et al., 2006; Rosenblatt, Shapira-Lishchinsky, & Shirom, 2010) have showed that teachers tended to be disproportionally absent on certain days of the week (in particular, before or after the weekend), thus indicating shirking behavior.

Ethical Aspects of Teacher Turnover and Attrition

As noted above, every person has the legitimate right to choose her/his workplace and to realize his/her personal abilities. Nevertheless, leaving one school for another (turnover), or leaving the educational system (attrition), can harm the school if the school has invested time and money in training the teacher who leaves, while also having a difficult time in finding a replacement. The harm is even worse if the teacher transfers her/his knowledge to a competing school, to a competing network, or outside of the educational system, while reducing the morale in his/her previous school because s/he left the job (Shapira-Lishchinsky, 2013b).

In sum, because voluntary withdrawal behaviors, such as lateness, absence, turnover, and attrition, potentially include unethical facets. The book's approach is that these unethical behaviors may reflect a response to school practices perceived by teachers as unethical and operating against teachers' rights and welfare.

Chapter 17

The Relationship between Organizational Ethics and Teachers' Withdrawal Behaviors

The main theory that explains the relationship between ethical predictors and withdrawal behaviors is the Theory of Planned Behavior that was developed by Ajzen and Fishbein (Ajzen, 2012; Ajzen & Fishbein, 2005). This theory assumes that the person's behavior is a result of a cognitive process that has, at its basis, an intention to behave in a certain way. This intention will determines if the person will or will not engage in the behavior. According to the theory, teachers' perceptions are related to their attitudes and these relationships may impact their behavior, such as decreasing voluntary tardiness, voluntary absence, turnover, or attrition. These perceptions concerning work lead to positive or negative attitudes, which lead to their respective behaviors. So, for example, teachers' perceptions and negative attitudes toward their schools will lead to negative behaviors via the increase of withdrawal behaviors.

Below are a few examples which can demonstrate the relationship between different dimensions of organizational ethics and teachers' withdrawal behaviors.

Ethical Climate and Teachers' Withdrawal Behaviors

The theoretical rationale for exploring the relationship that exists between the ethical climate in the school and teachers' withdrawal behaviors comes from the literature that has focused on the link between school ethics and volitional teacher behavior. School ethics relates to the moral distinction between good and bad employee behavior. If negative norms characterize the school climate, teachers will often express and rationalize their poor behavior that reflects such negative norms. However, the opposite is also true: when the school climate is perceived as being a moral one, workers tend to refrain from engaging in unacceptable behavior, including withdrawal behaviors (Shapira-Lishchinsky & Even-Zohar, 2011). When teachers perceive that the school is characterized by a positive caring climate, it helps to increase teachers' commitment toward the goals and objectives of the school (Cullen et al., 2003). One result is that teachers will exhibit less withdrawal behaviors (Cohen, 2015).

International Aspects of Organizational Ethics in Educational Systems, 73–78
Copyright © 2018 by Emerald Publishing Limited
All rights of reproduction in any form reserved
doi:10.1108/978-1-78714-777-520181017

Research has shown that the more an organization's ethical climate is positive, for example, characterized by friendship and concern for employees, work performances will increase. On the other hand, a climate that mainly focuses on achieving the organization's goals will lead to a decrease in the individual's performance (Chen, Chen, & Liu, 2013; Wang & Hsieh, 2013). This decrease in the employee's performance will be expressed in different withdrawal behaviors (Kanten & Ülker, 2013; Vardaman, Gondo, & Allen, 2014). In the school context, concern and care for the needs of the teachers contributes to the social solidarity in the organization. Teachers in this environment are more dedicated and committed to the school's goals. Therefore, it appears as if these teachers tend to be less tardy, less absent, and leave the workplace less than others (Rosenblatt & Shapira-Lishchinsky, 2017).

Greenlee and Brown's (2009) study raised the point that the school administration's concern and support of the teachers' work can contribute to a lower level of turnover and attrition. Other studies have shown that teachers' perceptions of the ethical climate are important to the success of the school. For example, it was found that the more teachers perceive the ethical climate in the school as characterized by concern, the rate of turnover and attrition decreases in relation to schools in which there is a lower level of perception of the ethical climate of concern (DeAngelis, Wall, & Che, 2013; Simon & Johnson, 2013).

Previous studies (e.g., Schneider, González-Romá, Ostroff, & West, 2017; Wallace et al., 2016) showed that perceptions of school climate characterized by caring for teachers were negatively related to withdrawal behaviors. A formal ethical climate, which stresses the organizational rules and procedures, may also be related to teachers' withdrawal behaviors. When teachers perceive that school principals are highly concerned with rules and regulations, they tend to exhibit less deviant behavior, such as coming late to class or missing school, in order to avoid being disciplined for their behaviors. Furthermore, ethical rules and norms are means of organizational socialization. Teachers learn how they are expected to behave in the school by taking note of the beliefs and principles that are respected and rewarded, and by taking note of the behaviors which are punished (Shapira-Lishchinsky & Raftar-Ozery, 2016).

Breach of the Psychological Contract and Teachers' Withdrawal Behaviors

The psychological contract includes beliefs related to the mutual commitment that exists between the teacher and the school's administration. A breach of a psychological contract is defined as the failure of the administration to fulfill its obligations toward its staff (Cohen, 2015). The more that a teacher feels that a breach was serious, s/he will tend to engage in more serious withdrawal behaviors. The teacher may first come to work late; afterwards, s/he may be absent or even leave, that is, the teacher may feel that the seriousness of the breach of the psychological contract is congruent with the withdrawal behaviors in which s/he decided to engage (Wang & Hsieh, 2013). For example, previous research has related breach of a psychological contract to absences (Pate & Scullion, 2016) and to turnover (Clinton & Guest, 2014).

Nevertheless, it has also been found that the perception of a breach of contract by an employee can impact his/her attitudes but not necessarily his/her behavior. This finding has been explained by the fact that employees' behaviors are also dependent on additional factors, such as the conditions of the labor market, the perception regarding the stability or instability of the workplace as well as the attitudes regarding colleagues and the sense of pride in working in a certain profession (Arshad, 2016). Therefore, it is possible that teachers who perceive a breach of psychological contract, for example, concerning promotion, will not actually engage in withdrawal behaviors due to the fear of beginning to work at a new place without the occupational security that usually characterizes the teaching profession. Another possible reason can be tied to the state of the labor market, which makes it difficult for former teachers to find alternative work that meshes with their skills at a higher salarylevel than usually offered by the educational system (Shapira-Lishchinksy & Tsemach, 2014).

Organizational Justice and Teachers' Withdrawal Behaviors

Organizational justice is deeply embedded in equity theory (Adams, 1965; Greenberg, 1990). Research, which has been carried out on organizational justice has consistently demonstrated that employees expect decisions made in their organizations to be fair. As a result, they will have adverse reactions to their workplaces when/if they believe that the decision-makers made unjust decisions about them (Greenberg & Colquitt, 2013). If we look at the issue this way, adoption of withdrawal behaviors is one way to restore an inequitable employment relationship. The traditional equity theory, which is rooted in the cognitive dissonance theory (Hinojosa, Gardner, Walker, Cogliser, & Gullifor, 2017), has hypothesized that when an individual feels that there is injustice, this produces in her/him a negative emotional state. This tension is thought to reflect the motive for the individual to reduce the inequity and the associated negative feelings that accompany the injustice. As a result, workers may perceive time away from work as one very good method for simultaneously lowering their investments and for gaining more valued non-work outcomes (Carpenter & Berry, 2017).

It might also be helpful to consider the psychological contract as a theoretical framework for understanding how teachers' perceptions of organizational justice and withdrawal behaviors relate to one another. A psychological contract is an individual's beliefs regarding the terms and conditions of a reciprocal exchange agreement (Montes, Rousseau, & Tomprou, 2015). It is a fundamental component in the beliefs and experiences that workers have in relation to their workplace and jobs (Robinson & Morrison, 2000). From the worker's perspective, a psychological contract is breached when s/he perceives that the employer is not living up to one or more of his/her obligations (Alcover, Rico, Turnley, & Bolino, 2017).

The emotional theory proposes that people feel frustration and anger when they perceive that someone is demeaning them, and this anger is associated with a behavioral response (Dalgleish & Power, 2000). As a result, people may respond to violations of psychological contracts with anger. This can lead to the employees engaging in work violations of their own. Teachers, similar to employees in other fields who experience injustice at their jobs, may see work injustices as a breach of the psychological contract, and hence become angry. This negative feeling in turn, can come to be expressed in withdrawal behaviors (Zimmerman, Swider, Woo, & Allen, 2016).

Although distributive and procedural unfairness are perceived as being related to each other (Lucas, Kamble, Wu, Zhdanova, & Wendorf, 2016; Organ & Ryan, 1995), we see each of these as having a unique relationship to absenteeism, which can be explained by the withdrawal process. Let us take the case of distributive justice. Teachers will perceive that their schools are unjust when they feel that there is an imbalance, that is, they are contributing more than what they are receiving (Robinson & Morrison, 2000). The result will be that teachers will reduce their efforts to match their work with organizational rewards. Teachers who feel that such an injustice exists, will also tend more to engage in withdrawal behaviors than teachers who do not have such a perception. In addition, research has shown that teachers who felt relatively disadvantaged in terms of reward distribution more frequently withdrew from work than educators who perceived distributive justice (Shapira-Lishchinsky, 2016).

Although there has not been as much empirical research on the topic of procedural justice and teachers' withdrawal behaviors, it can be hypothesized that these two concepts will be similarly connected to each other. Workers may perceive low levels of procedural justice at their places of employment as a violation of their psychological contract. As a result, they can express their opposition to the injustices by engaging in more withdrawal behaviors (Bal, de Lange, Ybema, Jansen, & van der Velde, 2011).

The psychological contract between the teachers and the school's administration is not a written contract; however, it contains beliefs and expectations that connect to the mutual commitment between the teacher and the administration. When the actual outcome is perceived as incongruent with the expectations, the teacher is disappointed due to her/his perception that the school did not treat her/him fairly (Cohen, 2015).

Studies have shown that the perception of a breach of a psychological contract is related to the perception of procedural and distributive injustice (Piccoli & De Witte, 2015; Rodwell & Gulyas, 2013). For example, when considering distributive justice, the violation of promises prevents the teacher from enjoying rewards that s/he expected based on her/his perception of distributive justice. The teacher will perceive that there was procedural injustice, for example, in the way that roles were unfairly divided in the school. This way the psychological contract also connects the teacher and the principal –both sides mutually contribute to the school if they fulfill their obligations. The breach of the contract weakens the connection between them. The injured side, which is usally the teachers' side, loses its faith in the system. As a result, the teacher withdraws from her/his work in order to repair the injustice (Wang & Hsieh, 2013).

For example, if the teacher feels that the psychological contact with her was breached, since she is not promoted to other roles in spite of her important contribution to the school and its students, she will regain the balance of the psychological contract by investing less in the school by engaging in different withdrawal behaviors. In this way, there will be congruence between her low level of investment and not being promoted (Shapira-Lishchinsky & Raftar-Ozery, 2016).

Tendency to Misbehave and Teachers' Withdrawal Behaviors

Many researchers perceive withdrawal behaviors of tardiness and absence as a response to the general tendency of misbehavior in organizations (Rosenblatt, Shapira-Lishchinksy, & Shirom, 2010; Vardi & Weitz, 2016). In the context of school, teachers develop norms that are rooted in the school, or in more general social values, which accept the reoccuring phenomenon of not taking work seriously. As a result of acceptance of these norms, teachers may be tardy or not come to work at all. The teachers perceive that since there is an atmosphere of withdrawal in the school and that withdrawal behaviors are common, they do not need to make attempts to come to work. Furthermore, it is also possible that if the teacher perceives negative behaviors toward the workplace as being acceptable, this can lead the teacher to devaluate the processes taking place in the school. As a result, the teacher may engage in misbehavior, such as absences and attrition (Shapira-Lishchinsky & Raftar-Ozery, 2016).

In the literature, the tendency for misbehavior is described as the willingness of employees to accept behaviors that might harm the organizational or social norms. This definition does not include the behaviors themselves (Linstead, Maréchal, & Griffin, 2014). Vardi and Weitz (2016) assert that, today, the tendency for misbehavior is an integral part of everyday organizational life. In other words, it is neither rare nor marginal behavior. As a result, teachers may accept colleagues' behaviors, such as tardiness or absenteeism, as a given, and not as something that is extraordinary, including the inadequate functioning that accompanies such behaviors. This might influence teachers to also engage in such behaviors in the future and to decrease their investment of time in the school because of these behaviors (Shapira-Lishchinsky & Tsemach, 2014).

The literature presents a number of examples of the tendency to misbehave in different organizations that are also relevant to the educational systems. For example: (1) damaging property – for example, improper use of technological equipment, such as shutting down computers at the end of the work day; (2) harming the process – for example, absences and tardiness of school teachers which harm the learning process of the students; and (3) political harm – for example, gossiping about colleagues and creating conflict groups in the teacher's lounge (Ben-Sasson & Somech, 2015).

The literature also relates to the internal, organizational impacts and to the external impacts on the tendency to engage in misbehavior. Vardi and Weitz (2016) perceive the tendency to misbehave as being influenced by two factors – norms which develop in the organization, and norms that are anchored in more general social values. In relation to the educational system, according to general social norms, there is a tendency to accept the teacher's explanation that s/he was late arriving at school due to a doctor's appointment. However, there will not be a tendency to accept the teacher's explanation that s/he was late getting to school since s/he went shopping at the mall instead of coming to teach. In a similar manner, given that the teaching profession is a women's profession, there are accepted internal norms that pregnant teachers can be absent due to doctors' appointments. However, in the private sector, these absences will be accepted to a lesser degree, since the norm will be that these appointments should be scheduled after work hours.

Chapter 18

Organizational Commitment as a Mediator between Organizational Ethics' Perceptions and Teachers' Withdrawal Behaviors

Up to this point, the direct relationships between the ethical perceptions and the different withdrawal behaviors were presented. In this chapter, I present the rationale for the existence of the mediator, organizational commitment, which links ethical perceptions to different withdrawal behaviors.

Organizational Commitment

Organizational commitment describes the relationship between the teacher and the school, a relationship that includes a strong belief in the school, the acceptance of the school's goals and values, the investment of effort in the school, and a strong desire to remain in the school (Choi, Oh, & Colbert, 2015). The perceptions that are expected to contribute to organizational commitment are those perceptions that increase the likelihood that the teacher will feel that the workplace is characterized by ethical and just processes (Fu & Deshpande, 2014).

Handbook of Employee Commitment by Meyer and Espinoza (2016) relate to three kinds of organizational commitment:

Affective commitment – This relates to employees who have an emotional connection with the organization, who identify with it, and are involved in it. Employees who have an affective commitment remain in the organization because they want to stay. In the educational system, teachers may perceive the level of affective commitment as high, for example, if they chose the teaching profession as a way to reach self-actualization by working in schools (Shapira-Lishchinsky, 2013b).

Normative commitment – This relates to the sense of commitment on the part of the employee to remain in the organization. Workers with this kind of

International Aspects of Organizational Ethics in Educational Systems, 79–81
Copyright © 2018 by Emerald Publishing Limited
All rights of reproduction in any form reserved
doi:10.1108/978-1-78714-777-520181018

commitment remain because they feel obligated to stay. In the educational system, teachers may perceive their commitment as being high if they believe that they can make a significant contribution to the school and be effective in the educational system (Shapira-Lishchinsky, 2009a).

Continuance commitment – This relates to the "price" that the employee pays if s/he leave the organization. Employees with such a commitment remain in the organization since they need to, or because they have no other choice. In the educational system, teachers with a high level of this kind of commitment may perceive that the teaching profession is the only alternative they have to provide for their family. Therefore, if they leave, they will not be able to find alternative work (Shapira-Lishchinsky, 2012).

According to Meyer, Morin, and Vandenberghe (2015), the dimensions of these types of commitments complement one another. An employee can simultaneously reach different levels of differentkinds of commitments. Some of the employees may feel continued commitment, that is, a strong need to remain in the organization, as well as normative commitment – a strong obligation to remain in the organization – but they do not wish to remain, that is, they have low affective commitment. Others may feel a strong desire to remain in the organization, but do not feel the need or commitment to do so. As a result, commitment to an organization includes and reflects different dimensions of commitments. According to multiple commitment, as well, people in organizations are exposed to more than one kind of commitment at a given point in time; therefore, their behavior is influenced by a number of commitments, not just one (Cohen, 2014).

Previous studies have shown that the dimension of affective commitment is more dominant than normative commitment for predicting different withdrawal behaviors (Cohen, 2003; Meyer, Stanley, Jackson, McInnis, Maltin, & Sheppard, 2012; Mowday, Porter, & Steers, 2013). These studies highlight that affective commitment, which reflects the desire to belong to the organization, is more significant than normative commitment, which is the obligation to belong to the organization, when explaining different withdrawal behaviors. These studies explain that the worker who *desires* to belong to the organization will put in more of an effort than a worker who *feels* the obligation to belong. Therefore, s/he will exhibit less withdrawal from his/her work in comparison to the employee who remains solely because of her/his feeling of obligation (Casimir, Ngee Keith Ng, Yuan Wang, & Ooi, 2014; Morin, Meyer, McInerney, Marsh, & Ganotice, 2015).

The Mediating Effect of Organizational Commitment

Research that I have conducted over the last decade (Shapira-Lishchinsky, 2009a, 2009b, 2012; Shapira-Lishchinsky & Even-Zohar, 2011) has shown that organizational commitment can mediate the different dimensions of organizational ethics perceptions and different withdrawal behaviors among teachers. Additional studies that support this approach are presented below. I focus on the relationships that exists between the different dimensions of organizational ethics perceptions and organizational commitment, and between organizational commitment and different withdrawal behaviors.

Relationship between the Perceptions of Organizational Ethics and the Attitude of Organizational Commitment

Ethical climate and organizational commitment: The work environment characterized by friendliness and social responsibility between the teachers encourages teachers to develop positive emotions for members of the school. As a result, this will increase the perception of affective commitment to the school (Cullen, Parboteeah, & Victor, 2004; Ruiz-Palomino, Martínez-Cañas, & Fontrodona, 2013).

Organizational justice and organizational commitment: The more the teachers feel that their investment in the school is higher than what they receive in return, they will tend to feel less connected, and their level of commitment to the school will decrease (Chockalingam & Deniz, 2002; Gelens, Dries, Hofmans, & Pepermans, 2013).

Relationship between the Attitude of Organizational Commitment and Withdrawal Behaviors

Organizational commitment and tardiness: Teachers who have a high level of commitment to the school hope to continue in the school, believe in the school's values, and are willing to put in an effort in order to express these stances. One of the expressions of this is the effort to arrive at work on time. As a result, previous studies have found negative relationships between the perception of organizational commitment and tardiness (Dishon-Berkovits & Koslowsky, 2002).

Organizational commitment and absenteeism: Teachers with a low level of organizational commitment consciously – or unconsciously – express negative attitudes toward absenteeism from the school (Tenhiälä et al., 2013). In comparison, teachers with a high level of organizational commitment will avoid being absent. This is how they will express their desire to continue to belong to the school (Hassan, Wright, & Yukl, 2014). Furthermore, the teacher who feels that her/his investment is higher than what s/he receives, will feel less of a connection and less of a commitment to the school, and as a result will be absent from work (Burton, Lee, & Holtom, 2002; Kehoe & Wright, 2013).

Organizational commitment and turnover/attrition: Teachers who feel that the degree of their investment in the school is higher than what they receive in return, will feel less connected and less obligated to the school. As a result, they will have a higher tendency to leave the school, and do so, if they find suitable conditions (Tarigan & Ariani, 2015; Yücel, 2012).

Chapter 19

The Relationships between Personal and Organizational Characteristics and Teachers' Withdrawal Behaviors

Most of the studies that have been conducted until now have focused on personal background variables, such as age, gender, seniority in the school and the holding of position, and organizational variables that include the size of the school and its regulations/procedures. I now present details of these variables and their relationships to teachers' withdrawal behaviors.

Personal Characteristics

Age

Throughout the world, the burden of childcare, caring for a sick child at home, or the task of dropping off children at their nursery schools and schools before work, mainly falls on younger teachers. As a result, previous studies have found that younger teachers tend to be late more often and have higher rates of abseenteism than older teachers (Shapira-Lishchinksy, 2007, 2009a).

Moreover, it appears as if commitment to the school increases with age due to the difficulties in finding alternate employment or due to the high level of satisfaction from the school. These lead the teachers to remain in the school for a long time. In light of these findings, it is not surprising to find that many studies among teachers in different schools throughout the world point to the negative relationship between age and absences (Rosenblatt, Shapira-Lishchinsky, & Shirom, 2010; Tenhiälä et al., 2013).

Seniority

Previous studies have shown that teachers with many years of seniority tend to feel that they have a high level of employment security. As the seniority in the school increases, the sense of employment security also increases. As a result, if an educational network decreases its teaching staff, it will tend to first fire the newer teachers.

International Aspects of Organizational Ethics in Educational Systems, 83–86
Copyright © 2018 by Emerald Publishing Limited
All rights of reproduction in any form reserved
doi:10.1108/978-1-78714-777-520181019

As a result, teachers with a high level of seniority do not try as hard and also tend to be late more often or absent than younger teachers (Shapira-Lishchinsky, 2013b).

Turnover appears to occur for a different reason. As seniority increases, teachers feel a higher level of commitment to the school (Shapira-Lishchinsky & Rosenblatt, 2009b). This is due to their decision to keep working in the school, or because, with the increase in seniority, the employment options outside of teaching decrease. As a result, teachers with many years of seniority do not tend to leave employment at their schools (Loeb, Miller, & Wyckoff, 2015).

Gender

It appears that the differences in tardiness and absences among men and women can be explained by the importance of work. In many countries in the world, there is a social expectation from the men that work will be central in their lives, more than for women. This is expressed, for example, in the higher pay that men receive. There is a social expectation that women will be responsible for the other or additional roles, which do not have financial rewards, such as child care (Roth, Purvis, & Bobko, 2012).

For this reason, since more women work in educational systems throughout the world than men, gender may influence withdrawal behaviors of teachers. Women who perceives as responsible for caring for their children, or who have other commitments, are sometimes forced to be late or to miss work altogether. Therefore, they will be late or miss work more than their male partners who work outside the educational system. This is due to the perception of the centrality of work, which is often expressed by the lower salaries that women receive, in comparison to their male partners (Shapira-Lishchinsky, 2009a).

When considering attrition, it is also possible that in educational systems throughout the world, in which the majority of employees are women, we can find "sisterhood." This phenomenon leads the women to perceive their school experiences as more positive than male teachers, thus improving their attitudes toward the school. As a result, they are less likely than the men to leave their positions in the educational system. It is also possible that this "sisterhood" pushes the male teachers out of the system since the men have different interests and since they do not feel a sense of belonging with the women (Shapira-Lishchinsky & Raftar-Ozery, 2016).

Roles in School

The assumption is that teachers who have special roles, will be satisfied with their work; therefore, they feel commitment to the organization. As a result, their rate of withdrawal behaviors will be lower than that of people who do not have special roles or functions. Previous research in educational systems has shown that an increase in role status is tied to a lower level of teachers' absences (Rosenblatt & Shirom, 2006).

Concerning tardiness – in my studies, it was found that the level of tardiness among teachers holding positions in the school was higher than among teachers who did not have a special position (Shapira-Lishchinsky, 2007). When attempting to explain this phenomenon, we found that teachers who hold school positions need to fulfill their educational functions between classes. For example, they need to take care of pressing disciplinary problems that cannot be dealt with at a later time. Therefore, at times, when a teacher takes care of disciplinary problems, this takes longer than the break, causing her/him to get to class late (Shapira-Lishchinsky & Raftar-Ozery, 2017; Shapira-Lishchinsky & Tsemach, 2014).

Organizational Characteristics

School Size

There is no clear relationship between school size and teachers' withdrawal behaviors. There have been Studies which found a positive relationship between school size and the frequency of teachers' absences and tardiness (e.g., Rosenblatt & Shirom, 2005). However, other studies did not find significant relationships between school size and different withdrawal behaviors (Shapira-Lishchinsky & Raftar-Ozery, 2016; Shapira-Lishchinsky & Tsemach, 2014). It is possible that these different results can be explained by differences in the levels of survelliance of teacher tardiness and absenteesim in the different ownership styles of the educational networks (i.e., public versus private) and the different educational levels (elementary, middle, and high schools), which are characterized by different sizes.

For example, in many large educational networks in different countries, it is customary to generate teacher absentee reports at least once a year. These reports, which are submitted to school principals, note the frequency of school-wide absenteeism in relation to other schools in the network, while retaining anonymity of the other schools. As a result, there is a good possibility that the school administration will keep track of the frequency of teacher absenteeism in light of the fact that such absenteeism is one of the measures of school effectiveness examined by the supervisors in the schools network. Moreover, the administrations of big schools are aware of the fact that, in the large schools, there is a feeling that absences of lone teachers are not noticed. As a result, they need to employ some kind of control to ensure that the frequency of teacher absenteeism will decrease. To the best of my knowledge, in many elementary schools in the world, which are smaller, no such reports are generated. Therefore, it is possible that the teachers in these school levels exploit the absence of tracking or the forgiving and intimate relationships that characterize small to medium-sized schools concerning tardiness or absenteeism.

Behavioral Regulations, Procedures, and Norms

Studies that have been undertaken across different nations provide evidence that school regulations and procedures may determine teachers' behaviors. According to the socialization model of the employee in organizations, workers' behaviors are mainly influenced by the socialization processes of the individuals in the organization. For example, in one school, a teacher who is late for work will not

Fig. 19.1:   Organizational Commitment as a Moderator of Organizational
Ethical Perceptions and Teachers' Withdrawal Behaviors.
(© Susannah Levin 2018).

receive any response for such behavior from the school, while in another school, the tardiness will be noted and the teacher will be reprimanded. As a result, different enforcement modes concerning tardiness in different schools can influence the rates of a teacher's tardiness (Johns & Al Hajj, 2015). Previous research found that tracking the teachers' reports and setting unequivocal and clear procedures concerning teacher absenteeism can lower the school rate of teachers' absences. These researchers emphasize the importance of administrative publishing and enforcement of the procedures (Duflo, Hanna, & Ryan, 2012; Santisi, Magnano, Hichy, & Ramaci, 2014).

In light of this review, Fig. 19.1 illustrates that in the school context, ethical organizational perceptions, which include ethical climate, organizational justice, psychological contract, and tendency to misbehave, relate to attitudes of organizational commitment. These, in turn, relate to withdrawal behaviors of tardiness, absenteeism, turnover, and attrition. The model further relates to the role of personal background characteristics, such as age, gender, seniority in school, and holding a position, and organizational background characteristics, such as school size and school procedures.

Chapter 20

Withdrawal Behaviors and Organizational Citizenship Behavior

Organizational citizenship behavior (OCB) refers to contributions made by employees to their workplace, beyond their formal obligations (Organ, 1988; Somech & Drach-Zahavy, 2000). OCB focuses on behaviors that, while they surpass expectations, are important and may even be crucial for an organization's survival. In other words, OCB is an extra-role behavior (Vigoda-Gadot, Beeri, Birman, & Somech, 2007). These behaviors do not only take place within an organization, but also include actions directed toward or perceived as beneficial to the organization (Van Dyne & LePine, 1998).

Organizational citizenship behavior was initially conceptualized by Organ (1988) as an individual discretionary behavior, which is neither directly nor explicitly recognized by the official reward system and that, in the aggregate, supports and helps the organization to run smoothly. We conceptualize OCB as being comprised facilitating behaviors that support the social fabric of an organization; however, they are not part of the job's fundamental tasks (Organ, 1997).

In the contexts of schools, OCB reflects contributions that teachers freely make or hold back, while understanding that their behaviors will neither lead to sanctions nor rewards (DiPaola & Tschannen-Moran, 2014). According to Somech and Drach-Zahavy (2000), OCB has three dimensions: (a) extra-role behavior toward the students (e.g., teachers will remain in the classroom during breaks to talk/listen to students); (b) extra-role behavior toward the staff (e.g., teachers will engage in activities that include sharing and cooperation); and (c) extra-role behavior toward the school as a unit (e.g., teachers will plan and run social activities for the school).

Somech and Drach-Zahavy (2000) found that while extra-role behavior toward the team is mainly expressed in helping colleagues, extra-role behavior toward the organization is usually manifested in initiating activities for the entire school. OCBs are becoming increasingly important for organizations because job descriptions cannot describe all of the behaviors needed for organizations to realize their goals (Van Peren, van den Berg, & Willering, 1999). Today, given that schools are being reorganized in a number of significant ways (e.g., Malaklolunthu & Shamsudin, 2011; Priestley, Miller, Barrett, & Wallace, 2011), only doing what was

International Aspects of Organizational Ethics in Educational Systems, 87–89
Copyright © 2018 by Emerald Publishing Limited
All rights of reproduction in any form reserved
doi:10.1108/978-1-78714-777-520181020

advertised in the job description's defined roles is not enough to optimize school effectiveness. Therefore, over time, schools have become increasingly dependent on teachers who do much more than fulfill their formal job requirements. In other words, they actively engage in OCB (Somech & Drach-Zahavy, 2000).

The idea that withdrawal behaviors can only be thought of as being harmful to the school and OCB will always benefit the school (e.g., Dineen, Lewicki, & Tomlinson, 2006; Lee & Allen, 2002; Sackett, 2002; Sackett, Berry, Wiemann, & Laczo, 2006) has led researchers to assume that these types of behaviors present separate performance spheres. As a result, people who usually take part in one type will avoid engaging in the other. For example, when an employee engages in the OCB by arriving at work before one has to be formally there, without missing a day, s/he will not engage in an opposite withdrawal behavior of being tardy or absent. Moreover, empirical and theoretical research on the antecedents of withdrawal behaviors and OCB usually show opposite relationships. For example, two studies came to the conclusion that employees, who are satisfied with their work conditions, are more likely to demonstrate OCB and less likely to engage in withdrawal behaviors (Dalal, 2005; Fox, Spector, & Miles, 2001).

However, this view of dichotomy between OCB and withdrawal behaviors may oversimplify the underlying processes that lead individuals to engage in such behaviors. Research has shown that one antecedent, such as stress, can cause voluntary absenteeism and OCB (e.g., Miles, Borman, Spector, & Fox, 2002). Furthermore, there have also been reported cases in which highly productive people also manifest withdrawal behaviors (Sackett, 2002). For example, in a school setting, we can find instances of a teacher who often organizes impressive social activities for the school, while also being absent during different times.

It has also been found that withdrawal behaviors do not necessarily arise from negative perceptions and attitudes (Hackett & Bycio, 1996; Staw & Oldham, 1978). For example, the conservation of resources theory avers that people will try to obtain, protect, and foster their resources while also limiting threats to the resources they possess (Hobfoll, 2001). Thus, withdrawal behaviors can be seen as actually providing employees with a needed break. In other words, workers do not necessarily withdraw every now and then because of negative perceptions and attitudes they hold concerning their workplaces. Rather, if teachers can withdraw for a limited amount of time, this may help them return to work with new energies and higher motivation. The end result will be increased school effectiveness.

Therefore, according to this logic, OCB and withdrawal behaviors do *not* represent distinct performance domains. Rather, we should think about OCB and withdrawal behaviors as being different points on a single continuum (e.g., Bennett & Stamper, 2001; Sackett et al., 2006). Adopting such a perspective makes it possible for us to position performances on the same scale, which is illustrated in Fig. 20.1. These are situated between withdrawal behaviors, which are usually perceived as being negative, and the pole of OCB, which is usually considered positive.

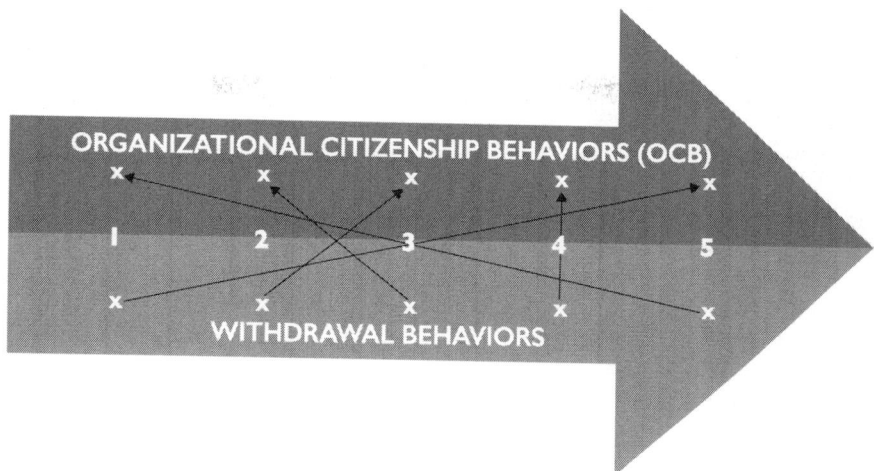

Fig. 20.1: The Relationship between Organizational Citizenship Behavior and Withdrawal Behaviors. (© Susannah Levin 2018).

Fig. 20.1 presents several optional cases, for example, a teacher who is relatively high in OCB and low in withdrawal behaviors; a teacher who is relatively high in withdrawal behaviors and low in OCB; and a teacher who is relatively high in both OCB and withdrawal behaviors.

Chapter 21

The Relationship between Organizational Ethics' Perceptions and Withdrawal and Citizenship Behaviors: A Summary of Updated Studies

In this chapter, I present a summary of several updated studies that explore the relationship between ethical predictors and withdrawal behaviors and organizational citizenship behaviors in different educational systems.

An Integrative Perspective: Teachers' Withdrawal Behaviors

This research (Shapira-Lishchinsky, 2010) explored the relationships between different dimensions of organizational ethics and a variety of withdrawal symptoms – tardiness, absences, and intent to leave the job. The participants in the study included 1,016 school teachers who worked in 35 high schools in Israel. In order to undertake the analysis, a joint model of GLIMMIX procedure of SAS was used, which simultaneously measured: (a) tardiness, using the negative binomial distribution; (b) absence, using the Poisson distribution; and (c) intent to leave the job, using the normal distribution. The results of the study showed that the different dimensions of organizational ethics were related to one another. It was found that the formal school climate and the distributive justice were negatively related to lateness. A caring climate was negatively related to frequency of absenteeism. Finally, procedural justice was negatively related to the teachers' intent to leave the workplace.

The results indicated a number of differences between ethical predictors – some might be due to extrinsic motivation factors while others might be due to intrinsic motivation factors. Regarding socio-demographic predictors: female teachers were found to be absent more than male teachers. However, they exhibited less intent to leave than their male counterparts. Teachers, who have many years of seniority, prefer absences over the intent to leave their job. Additionally, older teachers exhibit lower rates of tardiness and absence than younger ones.

This study also has practical implications: it is in the interest of the schools' leadership to develop an integrative approach, which will include ethics and

International Aspects of Organizational Ethics in Educational Systems, 91–94
Copyright © 2018 by Emerald Publishing Limited
All rights of reproduction in any form reserved
doi:10.1108/978-1-78714-777-520181021

socio-demographic factors. This can help reduce teachers' withdrawal behaviors. This approach can be achieved in a number of ways – through the development of training programs, clear rules, incentives, and through the delegation of power. Furthermore, this research was original in that it offered an integrative framework by taking into consideration different aspects of ethics, withdrawal behaviors, and socio-demographic predictors.

Developing a Scale for Teachers' Acceptance of Absenteeism

This study (Shapira-Lishchinsky & Ishan, 2013) both developed and validated a specific measure of an attitude toward teachers' absenteeism that can predict such behavior more accurately than general measures of job attitudes. The participants, which were comprised 443 teachers from 21 high schools in Israel, participated in the research that had two phases. In the first phase, they anonymously answered questionnaires that tapped both their general attitudes and their specific attitudes concerning "absenteeism acceptance." In the second phase, each teacher submitted copies of her/his half-year absenteeism records, six months after the first phase of the research ended.

The analyses used CFA to cross validate the different job attitude measures. Results confirmed the construct validity of "absenteeism acceptance" through convergent and discriminant validity. Relatively weak negative relationships were found to exist between "absenteeism acceptance" and the general attitudes toward the job. The criterion validity and predictive validity of the new measure were confirmed by inter-correlations. These inter-correlations were relatively stronger between "absenteeism acceptance" and the two measures of absenteeism (frequency and duration) than between the general job attitudes and these two measures. Quasi-Possion regressions indicated that "absenteeism acceptance" is a better predictor for both absenteeism measures than other general job attitudes.

It was concluded that the new measure of "teachers' acceptance of absenteeism" can benefit schools and principals by helping them identify potential absenteeism antecedents. Such identification can then enable early intervention. While previous research on work absence mainly focused on general attitude antecedents, this study addressed a specific "absenteeism acceptance" measure. The results support the notion that this measure can be advantageous in both understanding and predicting voluntary absenteeism and is more precise than general attitude measures.

Predictors of Teachers' Absence and Citizenship Behaviors

The goal of this study, which was undertaken in 2016 (Shapira-Lishchinsky & Raftar-Ozery, 2016) was to explore the mediating role that "absenteeism acceptance" plays between different leadership styles and the school ethical climate on organizational citizenship behaviors and voluntary absence. Three hundred and four Israeli teachers, who were randomly selected from 304 mainstream and special education schools, were the participants. The model was analyzed using AMOS 18.0 software. The results showed that "absenteeism acceptance" partially mediated the relationship between transactional leadership, school ethical climate, and organizational citizenship behaviors. Furthermore, we learned that school ethical climate and transactional leadership positively predict organizational citizenship behaviors.

This study made a theoretical contribution to the literature, due to its integrative approach. While most studies on the topic have focused on a single leadership style, we concentrated on the role of "absenteeism acceptance," as a mediator between ethical aspects, such as school ethical climate and leadership styles, and teachers' behaviors such as voluntary absence and organizational citizenship behaviors. The research also makes a practical contribution: it recommends inclusion of principals' training programs, which will focus on transactional leadership and school ethical climate, since they have the potential to increase teachers' organizational citizenship behaviors in schools.

The Mediating Effect of Psychological Empowerment Between Teachers' Perceptions of Authentic Leadership and their Withdrawal and Citizenship Behaviors

This study (Shapira-Lishchinsky & Tsemach, 2014) explored the mediating role of psychological empowerment on authentic leadership, organizational citizenship behaviors, and different withdrawal behaviors among teachers. It employed the psychological model of perceptions–attitudes–behaviors. The sample was comprised 366 teachers who were drawn from 23 randomly selected schools in Israel. The study used a combination of self-reports and school records, which were taken at regular time intervals and which focused on lateness, absenteeism, and intent to leave – three well-known withdrawal behaviors. The model for the hierarchical data (teachers within schools), which encompassed latent and manifest variables, was analyzed using the Mplus statistical package applying to multilevel analysis.

The findings showed that "impact," a dimension of psychological empowerment, mediated the relationship between authentic leadership and organizational citizenship behaviors. However, the second dimension of psychological empowerment – "self-determination, meaning, and competence" – mediated the relationship between authentic leadership and frequency of absence. The results did not indicate a mediating relationship for psychological empowerment on authentic leadership and the withdrawal behaviors of tardiness and intent to leave.

This research helped improve the Ajzen and Fishbein (2005) model. While to date most studies that have explored withdrawal behaviors have centered on one dimension of withdrawal behaviors, and have not considered organizational citizenship behaviors, our study offered an integrative framework. It looked at the mediating role of psychological empowerment as an ongoing link between authentic leadership and a range of teachers' withdrawal behaviors and organizational citizenship behaviors. Results from this research should motivate principals to promote high standards of authentic leadership. This can help empower their teachers, increase organizational citizenship behaviors, and lower the rates of teacher absenteeism.

The Motivational Aspects of Citizenship Behavior and Misbehavior among Administrative and Supervision Staff in Ministry of Education

This research (Shapira-Lishchinsky & Levy-Gazenfrantz, 2015) investigated the motivational aspects that underpin citizenship behavior and misbehavior among administrative and supervision staff who are employed in the Israeli Ministry of Education. Based on the sequence theory, the study explored the relationship between motivational perceptions, intentions to behave, as well as two types of behaviors: organizational citizenship behavior and organizational misbehavior. The study participants, who were randomly selected from seven Israeli districts of the ministry, were comprised 307 administrative employees and 317 superintendents.

In order to address the research questions, the study combined self-reports and computer records of lateness, absenteeism, and turnover. The model was analyzed using the Mplus statistical package applied to multilevel analysis. The results indicate several mediating relationships: (a) Intent to leave was found to mediate the relationship between authentic leadership and lateness, in addition to the relationship between authentic leadership and citizenship behavior. (b) Intentions to engage in organizational citizenship behaviors were found to mediate the relationship between "impact" and "self-determination," which are the dimensions of psychological empowerment and organizational citizenship behavior.

It was concluded that this study expanded Ajzen and Fishbein's (2005) sequence theory by exploring the motivational perceptions that impact workers' organizational citizenship behaviors and organizational misbehaviors intentions and behaviors. The research results can encourage organizational leaders to aim for high standards of authentic leadership. This can have multiple effects: It can empower their employees, increase their organizational citizenship behaviors intentions, and reduce their organizational misbehaviors intentions.

Chapter 22

Analyzing the Relationship between Perceptions of Organizational Ethics and Teachers' Withdrawal Behaviors

In this chapter, I present questionnaires that I used in my research, and developed and updated, so that they would be relevant for educational systems. These questionnaires measure teachers' perceptions regarding different dimensions of organizational ethics and teachers' withdrawal behaviors.

Perceptions of Ethical School Climate

In my research, I often use a questionnaire that measures ethical school climate that comprises 15 items on a Likert scale of 1–5. This questionnaire was developed on the basis of an instrument used in business organizations (Cullen, Victor, & Bronson, 1993). Based on analyses of exploratory and confirmatory factors, I chose items that are relevant for diverse educational systems throughout the world.

In my studies (e.g., Shapira-Lishchinsky, 2013b; Shapira-Lishchinsky & Raftar-Ozery, 2016), two central dimensions were found: the caring ethical climate ($a = 0.86$) and the formal ethical climate ($a = 0.87$). The caring ethical climate (items 1–3 and 13–15 in the questionnaire given below) emphasizes values of concern for colleagues. Another factor is the formal ethical climate (items 12–14 in the questionnaire), which emphasizes compliance to rules and regulations connected to the professional field of teachers while being concerned with the school's effectiveness.

Questionnaire 22.1. Perceptions of Ethical School Climate

Here are a number of statements that represent the atmosphere in the school. Please circle the relevant answer.

International Aspects of Organizational Ethics in Educational Systems, 95–103
Copyright © 2018 by Emerald Publishing Limited
All rights of reproduction in any form reserved
doi:10.1108/978-1-78714-777-520181022

		Do Not Agree at All	Do Not Agree	Partially Agree	Fairly Agree	Highly Agree
1.	In this school, caring about the good of the teachers and students is the most important thing.	1	2	3	4	5
2.	In this school, they care about the well-being of the teachers and students.	1	2	3	4	5
3.	The teachers in this school see staff spirit as important.	1	2	3	4	5
4.	In this school, the teachers are expected to maintain the rules, above and beyond their personal considerations.	1	2	3	4	5
5.	In this school, maintaining the professional ethical code is a central consideration.	1	2	3	4	5
6.	In this school, it is expected that the teachers will strictly uphold professional standards.	1	2	3	4	5
7.	In this school, it is very important to follow procedures.	1	2	3	4	5
8.	In this school, each teacher is expected to uphold the decisions/rules.	1	2	3	4	5
9.	The teachers in this school strictly follow the school's policy.	1	2	3	4	5
10.	In this school, it is expected that, above all else, the teachers will be efficient in their work.	1	2	3	4	5
11.	Being efficient is the most important thing to do in this school.	1	2	3	4	5
12.	This school is always searching for the most efficient solutions.	1	2	3	4	5
13.	In this school, people care/have concern for one another.	1	2	3	4	5
14.	The main concern in this school is for the well-being of all teachers.	1	2	3	4	5
15.	In this school, when decisions are made, they take all the teachers into consideration.	1	2	3	4	5

Perceptions of Organizational Justice in Schools

In my research, I often use a questionnaire of organizational justice that has 13 items on a Likert scale of 1–5. The questionnaire was developed on the basis of questionnaires that were designed for organizations outside the educational systems (Moorman, 1991), and chooses items relevant for diverse educational systems throughout the world based on exploratory and confirmatory factors' analyses.

In my study (Shapira-Lishchinsky, 2012), this measurment was found to include two main dimensions: distributive justice – items 1–7, and procedural justice – items 8–13 (the questionnaire is given below). The reliabily of distributive justice was $a = 0.87$, and the reliability of procedural justice was $a = 0.94$.

Questionnaire 22.2. Perceptions of Organizational Justice in Schools

Below are given a number of statements that represent teachers' perceptions. Please indicate your degree of agreement with these statements.

	Don't Agree at All	Don't Agree	Partially Agree	Agree	Highly Agree
1. My teaching schedule is fair.	1	2	3	4	5
2. I think that my salary is fair.	1	2	3	4	5
3. I feel that the responsibility placed on me in school is basically fair.					
4. When I compare myself with others, in terms of compensation for my work, I feel satisfied.	1	2	3	4	5
5. I believe that the compensation I receive for my work reflects my contribution to the school.	1	2	3	4	5
6. The teachers in this school receive fair treatment, based on their personal needs.	1	2	3	4	5
7. The compensation that I receive for my work is fair because it fulfills my needs.	1	2	3	4	5
8. The decision-making process used by the principal is fair.	1	2	3	4	5

(*Continued*)

		Don't Agree at All	Don't Agree	Partially Agree	Agree	Highly Agree
9.	Before reaching a decision in school matters, the principal makes sure to hear the opinions of all of the teachers impacted by the issue.	1	2	3	4	5
10.	In order to reach a decision about a school issue, the principal collects precise information and data.	1	2	3	4	5
11.	The principal gives additional information to the teachers who ask for it.	1	2	3	4	5
12.	The school decisions are applied in a consistent manner for all the teachers affected by the decision.	1	2	3	4	5
13.	The teachers can appeal decisions made by the principal.	1	2	3	4	5

Perceived Psychological Contract Breach in Schools

In my studies, I have used a questionnaire for the perceived psychological contract breach in schools (Rosenblatt & Shapira-Lishchinsky, 2017). It has nine items on a Likert scale of 1–5. On the basis of exploratory and confirmatory factors analyses, the questionnaire was developed based on the questionnaires that were designed for organizations outside the educational systems (Moorman, 1991; Robinson & Morrison, 2000) by choosing and wording relevant items for diverse educational systems throughout the world. The reliability was found to be relatively high ($a = 0.92$).

Questionnaire 22.3. Perceived Psychological Contract Breach in Schools

To what extent do you agree with the following statements? Circle the answers that, in your opinion, best match your degree of agreement with each of the following items.

	Don't Agree at All	Don't Really Agree	Partially Agree	Fairly Agree	Highly Agree
1. Almost all of the promises the principal made me when I began working in the school have been kept up until now.	1	2	3	4	5
2. I feel very angry toward the school.	1	2	3	4	5
3. I feel betrayed by the school.	1	2	3	4	5
4. I didn't get all the compensation that the school administration promised me for my investment in the school.	1	2	3	4	5
5. I feel that my prinicpal came through with all of the promises that were made to me when I began working at the school.	1	2	3	4	5
6. I feel that the school breached the contract between us.	1	2	3	4	5
7. I feel frustrated by the way the school treats me.	1	2	3	4	5
8. Until now, my principal has done good work keeping his/her promises to me.	1	2	3	4	5
9. My school broke many promises made to me in spite of the fact that I fulfilled all of my jobs.	1	2	3	4	5

Perceptions of Tendency to Misbehave in Schools

In my research (Shapira-Lishchinsky, 2011), I have used a questionnaire that examines the tendency to misbehave in schools. This questionnaire has 17 items on a Likert scale from 1 to 5 and was based on a questionnaire developed for business organizations (Vardi, 2001) by choosing and phrasing relevant items for a variety of educational systems around the world. It was based on exploratory and confirmatory factors' analyses. The reliability of the questionnaire was high for educational systems, nearly $a = 0.90$.

In order to prevent bias due to social desirability, the respondents fill out the questionnaire on their perceptions toward inappropriate behavior in schools, in general, and do not answer if they tend to engage in such behaviors. The assumption is that if the respondents do not accept such behaviors, then their tendency to behave in such ways in school is low (Shapira-Lishchinsky & Even-Zohar, 2011).

Questionnaire 22.4. Perceptions of Tendency to Misbehave in Schools

The following statements help characterize different behaviors in schools. The questionnaire does not examine whether you or other teachers engage in such behaviors, but rather asks for your opinions about these behaviors. What is your opinion about the following behaviors in school? Please circle your answers.

	The Behavior is Completely Unacceptable to Me	The Behavior is Unacceptable	It Depends	I Support Such Behavior	I Strongly Support Such Behavior
1. Being late for school.	1	2	3	4	5
2. Leaving school before my work day is over.	1	2	3	4	5
3. Taking a longer than permissible break after the bell rings.	1	2	3	4	5
4. Being absent from school without a legitimate reason.	1	2	3	4	5
5. Being absent from school due to a medical issue, without actually being ill.	1	2	3	4	5
6. Making personal phone calls during class (including leaving the classroom for this).	1	2	3	4	5
7. Using the school's photocopier for personal reasons.	1	2	3	4	5

	The Behavior is Completely Unacceptable to Me	The Behavior is Unacceptable	It Depends	I Support Such Behavior	I Strongly Support Such Behavior
8. Taking care of things unconnected with education during the time you should be teaching.	1	2	3	4	5
9. Being negligent with school equipment.	1	2	3	4	5
10. Wasting the school's materials or budget.	1	2	3	4	5
11. Taking equipment home without permission (paper, staples, stapler, pens, etc.)	1	2	3	4	5
12. Getting benefits (presents) as compensation for favoring certain students.	1	2	3	4	5
13. Giving presents for showing favoritism.	1	2	3	4	5
14. Preferring certain students over others.	1	2	3	4	5
15. Providing deceptive reports (work hours, output etc.).	1	2	3	4	5
16. Acting against decisions made by the school's administration.	1	2	3	4	5
17. Taking lightly the school's rules about caution.	1	2	3	4	5

Measuring Teachers' Tardiness

In light of the research that I have conducted until now (Rosenblatt & Shapira-Lishichinsky, 2017; Shapira-Lishchinsky, 2017), I recommend measuring teachers' tardiness by the frequency of the rate of tardiness; in other words, the number of tardiness during 30 days before answering the questionnaire. I found that teachers can still remember what they did over the last 30 days and report the correct number of times they were late for work (Shapira-Lishchinsky, 2007; Shapira-Lishchinsky & Tsemach, 2014).

In my research on teachers' tardiness, I used a questionnaire that was developed on the basis of instruments that were constructed for organizations outside educational systems (Neal, Chapman, Ingersoll-Dayton, & Emloen, 1994), and worded the relevant items for a variety of educational systems throughout the world. I found that teachers perceive lateness as arriving at a class more than six minutes later from the time it was scheduled to begin. As a result, arriving to class five minutes late is not generally perceived in variety educational systems in the world as being late. Rather, it is seen as a logical time for getting organized to begin the class.

Below is given a self-report questionnaire for teachers that I often use in my studies, because of the reports about teachers' tardiness are not usually documented in most of the educational systems in the world.

Questionnaire 22.5. Teachers' Tardiness

During the last 30 days, how many times were you late for class? (For purpose of measurement, tardiness is defined as arriving late in class by six minutes or more after the bell.)

0   1   2   3   4   5   6   7   8   9

Other _____

If you reported for one or more times that you were late, what were the main reasons for your tardiness (please list according to their importance)

1. _____   2. _____   3. _____   4. _____

Measurement of Teachers' Absenteeism

Below follows a self-report questionnaire that I have used in many studies (Shapira-Lishchinsky, 2012; Shapira-Lishchinsky & Raftar-Ozery, 2016; Shapira-Lishchinsky & Tsemach, 2014). I compared the results with the reports from human resources department to strengthen the reliability of the measurement of teachers' absenteeism during the studied period. It is recommended to include a calendar to make it easier for the teachers filling out the questionnaire to remember when they missed work. Of course, it is important to change the names of the month in accordance with the period of the research, while making sure that the period was during the school year.

Questionnaire 22.6. Teachers' Absenteeism

I. Please estimate the rate of your absence and the reason for these absences during the last six months (October–March), not including reserve duty, maternity leave, holidays, and strikes of all of the teachers. It is recommended that you use the calendar of the academic year provided by the school/Ministry of Education/ your own or personal diary (e.g., your mobile phone).

Absences in October:	Absences in January:
1. Total: ____ days. Reason: _____	1. Total: ____ Reason: _____
2. Total: ____ days. Reason: _____	2. Total: ____ Reason: _____
3. Total: ____ days. Reason: _____	3. Total: ____ Reason: _____
Absences in November:	**Absences in February:**
1. Total: ____ days. Reason: _____	1. Total: ____ Reason: _____
2. Total: ____ days. Reason: _____	2. Total: ____ Reason: _____
3. Total: ____ days. Reason: _____	3. Total: ____ Reason: _____
Absences in December:	**Absences in March:**
1. Total: ____ days. Reason: _____	1. Total: ____ Reason: _____
2. Total: ____ days. Reason: _____	2. Total: ____ Reason: _____
3. Total: ____ days. Reason: _____	3. Total: ____ Reason: _____

Comment: If you were absent for a few days in a row, report the event as one absence (on one line).

II. What is the date that you are filling out this questionnaire? _____

III. Only if you do not remember (about question I):
During the last six months, I was absent for a total of _____ days, ____ number of times.

Measurement of Teachers Leaving Schools (Attrition/Turnover)

I recently developed a self-report questionnaire for teachers that asks for the reasons for quitting, and the character of the attrition/turnover. A similar questionnaire was found to be valid for school principals (Melon, 2018).

Questionnaire 22.7. Teachers Leaving Schools (Attrition/Turnover)

Please circle the correct answer. At the end of this work year:
I will leave teaching forever since I am retiring: Yes/No
I will leave teaching since I am taking early retirement: Yes/No
I will move to another school: Yes/No
I will have a promotion in the educational system: Yes/No
I will leave my school for this reason: _____

Chapter 23

Learner-Centered Education – Toward a Decrease in Teachers' Withdrawal Behaviors

Withdrawal behaviors of teachers, such as tardiness, absence, turnover, and attrition, may be perceived as critical when educational leaders, such as principals, vice principals, and supervisors, are presented with ethical dilemmas and conflicts that can be approached in different ways. Seminars and workshops that focus on ethical events, which relate to withdrawal behaviors, provide opportunities to ask how leaders respond to such events in school, the lessons they learn from such events, and what is taken into consideration, when seeking solutions. Based on the lessons the educational leaders have learned, the answer to these and other questions can improve professional judgment and help leaders use their judgment in the future dilemmas. In effect, it can be said that long-term learning takes place by analyzing critical events.

One of the strategies that can be used for addressing withdrawal behaviors of teachers is learner-centered education (LCE). An emphasis is placed on both the activism and reflection of the learner during the process and the diversity in the group (Schweisfurth, 2013). During the workshops, it is recommended to use the following strategies, characteristic of LCE: (a) encouragement of participants to ask questions about the ethical dilemmas and conflicts that they experience at work, which are due to teachers' withdrawal behaviors; (b) basing the seminar on participants' knowledge, which is a result of their professional experiences with withdrawal behaviors; (c) using dialogue during the process by engaging in group discussion about withdrawal behaviors that the participants have experienced; (d) exposing participants to stressors connected to withdrawal behaviors, by raising dilemmas and difficulties from the field and by attempting to deal with them and find solutions; and (e) developing critical thinking skills and creativity through rich interpersonal experiences that make it possible for the participants to learn about their leadership abilities, their interpersonal relationships, and their behavior in teams working on withdrawal behaviors. In this way, experiential learning can take place since participants learn that others need to cope with similar difficulties, that helping others empowers the participant who is providng the help, and that learning from the experiences of peers is fruitful. Furthermore, this learning takes place among peers in a safe space.

Here are some examples of recommendations of different critical events that can be used in seminars or workshops that are designed for educators in leadership

International Aspects of Organizational Ethics in Educational Systems, 105–106
Copyright © 2018 by Emerald Publishing Limited
All rights of reproduction in any form reserved
doi:10.1108/978-1-78714-777-520181023

roles such as principals, vice principals, and supervisors. These encounters are designed to provide tools for and knowledge about coping with withdrawal behaviors of educators and teachers.

Case 23.1. An Annual Report of Teachers' Absences

You are a principal of a school with 1,000 students. This school is part of a large educational network of 40 high schools. Your supervisor sent you an annual report of teachers' absences in which your school is the third highest with teacher absences in the network. Every principal in the network received the report, which includes a histogram with the rates of teachers' absences in his/her school, in comparison to anonymous columns of teachers' absences in the other schools in the network/system. The supervisor set up a meeting with you and the vice principal, in which you will explain to her what caused this high level of absences. What will you say in this meeting?

Case 23.2. Absence Frequency and Duration

You are a principal of a middle school that has 100 teachers. Two teachers were absent for nine days during the first semester. Donna was absent for nine consecutive days, and Rachel was absent for three days each time. You sent a personal report to both teachers showing for how many times s/he had been absent. You attached personal notes to Donna and Rachel, writing that you would be glad to meet separately with each one of them to discuss their absences. Donna and Rachel, who are representatives of the Teachers' Committee of the school, ask to meet with you together in order to talk about the reports and notes that you sent them, but not to others. What will you do? What will you say?

Case 23.3. Parental Involvment in Teachers' Absenteeism

Charlotte is a math teacher for the eighth grade in the school where you are a principal. She is often absent because of her young children's health issues. The parents have been complaining about her absences and are worried that their children will be missing out on material they need to know in high school. In addition, the parents talked to you about their worry that their children are not learning the material they need to pass the entrance exams to the city high schools. The parents have no complaints about the quality of Charlotte's teaching; they say that Charlotte is a professional teacher and is good at teaching the material when she comes to class. However they are not willing to accept that a teacher of such an important subject will miss so many lessons. You have set up a meeting with Charlotte to discuss the matter. She has told you that her husband cannot miss work because of children's illnesses; he has a senior position that demands his presence. Furthermore, she has no family members who can help out. As a result, she is forced to miss class. What will you say to her?

Chapter 24

Strategies for Minimizing Withdrawal Behaviors among Teachers

In this chapter, I focus on different strategies that are used at the school level, undertaken by the principals and administrations, and at the level of the departments of education and educational authorities, carried out at the functionaries' headquarters. These strategies, as detailed below, are relevant for different educational systems throughout the world. The strategies are based on the experiences of educational leaders and teachers who have held different positions, and on the studies that come from different places in the world on the topic. These strategies can be applied at the school level, as well as the level of the headquarters and districts and are categorized according to how much they care for the employees, or approach the issues from a formal standpoint.

Strategies at the School Level

Strategies Characterized by Care for the Teacher

- *Taking into consideration family characteristics*: If at all possible, it is good to be flexible when organizing the teaching schedule of single fathers and mothers, who have custody of their children. For example, in order to make it possible for these teachers to do their job without worry, it is recommended to give them a work schedulce in which they teach in the middle of the day, and not at the beginning. This is because of their responsibilities and obligations, for example, of having to drop the children off at their nursery schools and schools, or taking them to pediatrics' appointments, which are usually scheduled for the morning. Taking into consideration their unique family characteristics can decrease the number of times that these teachers are late for class, and lower their number of absences from school. The flexibility of the school's administration can also increase the teachers' satisfaction, as well as lower the rate of attrition of the teachers.
- *Decentralization of functions*: In schools, there is a tendency to distribute important functions/roles to a very small number of respected teachers. In these instances, it is recommended to offer opportunities to a large number of teachers in order to increase the significance of other teachers' contributions

International Aspects of Organizational Ethics in Educational Systems, 107–112
Copyright © 2018 by Emerald Publishing Limited
All rights of reproduction in any form reserved
doi:10.1108/978-1-78714-777-520181024

to the school. Such a decentralization process can increase the number of teachers who are committed to the school due to their meaningful educational work. This will result in a decrease in absence and lateness rates. In addition, the task load will divide more equally among a number of educators. As a result, there will be a decrease in the harm to the school, because there will be less instances of tardiness, absences or attrition.

- *Development of positive perceptions of the school climate*: The organization of workshops, both inside and outside the school, can help achieve this goal. In these workshops, it is important that the educators discuss ethical events, in experiential ways, that arose as a result of school activities. For example, they can analyze case studies of the events, or engage in simulations. These workshops have the potential to contribute to the airing of emotions and to the teachers and faculty becoming opened to receiving feedback on school processes. After these workshops, there are good chances that the ethical atmosphere in the school will improve. As a result, it is expected that the rates of tardiness, absences and attrition – among those who participated in the workshops – will decrease.

- *Transparency of processes involved in decision making in the school*: It is important that there be transparency in the processes taking place in the school. For example, if there is a need to appoint a teacher to a position, it is important that all of the teachers are made aware of the job search, and that the announcement includes the required skills and demands of the position. This will make it possible for interested teachers to submit their candidacy. In other words, the administration should not discreetly ask certain people if they are interested in the job. This mode of working can increase the motivation of teachers to advance within the school system, due to the knowledge that there are possibilities of promotion. In this way, the teachers will meet their deadlines and be punctual. This can also increase their presence in the school as well as their desire to continue working in the school.

- *Pairing a mentor-teacher with a teacher who has high potential of quitting his/her job*: The process of mentoring and support from both the professional aspect and the aspect of having insider knowledge of the educational system can lower frustrations, and ambiguity and uncertainty among young/new teachers. Such a process can also increase the meaning of the work in the school and, in this way, lessen the frequency of being late getting to class. It can also increase the teacher's presence in the school and the desire to continue working in the educational system.

- *Setting one-on-one meetings between the principal and the teachers at least once every three months*: The objective of these meetings is to discuss the teacher's progress, expectations that the sides have, and possibilities of improving the existing situation. These meeting may contribute to an increase in the perception of the significance/meaning of the job and empowerment of the teachers – both the younger and more experienced ones. In this way, it is possible to decrease the rate of tardiness, absences and the wish to leave the job at the school.

Strategies Characterized by Formality Toward the Teacher

- *Generation of a monthly personal teacher's report*: This report will be generated by the school's administrative staff and will document the score on the rate of monthly absences of the teacher, based on a measurement of the length of the absence and a measure of the frequency of absences. This will make it possible to see if the teacher's absences have voluntary characteristics, that is, if there are a number of absences. The generation of this report may encourage the teachers to decrease their absences since they will know that the administration is surveilling their absences and their frequencies. If a computerized system tracks teachers' tardiness (e.g., teachers punch a time clock), it is recommended to generate a similar report about the frequencies of tardiness to class.
- *Changing procedures concerning substitutes*: In many schools throughout the world, it is customary that if a teacher needs to go on leave for a relatively short period of time that could not be scheduled ahead of time, the teacher calls the school on the morning s/he will be gone to let them know that s/he will be absent. Then the school's administration needs to find a solution for his/her students. In a few schools in different countries, I found that teachers who announce that they will not be able to come to work that day have the responsibility of preparing learning materials for the subsitute teacher. This procedure facilitates the smooth continuation of the material by the substitute. It also encourages the teachers, who are interested in being absent from work due to voluntary reasons, to reconsider if it is possible to prevent the absence because of the effort needed to prepare material for the substitute teacher.
- *Refreshing and updating school procedures concerning tardiness and absence.* For example, The school can add a procedure about the teacher's obligation to report all absences to his/her direct superior in the school (e.g., the principal or the administrative manager). This procedure may lead the teacher to carefully consider absences due to the unpleasantness connected to having to report directly to one's superior.
- *Examination of the classrooms in which the teaching takes place.* In some countries, it is customary that the students in middle and high schools remain in their homerooms for their classes, while the teachers move between these classrooms. The students only change classrooms when they need equipment or materials available in a laboratory or workshop. In these latter lessons, the teachers wait for the students in the laboratories or workshops. The students come to these classrooms because they understand that the learning process is more relevant in spaces that are suited for these activities. Oftentimes, when teachers move between the classrooms, they enter late because they have been talking to students or with the administration about academic issues. At times, they are late because they were in conversation with someone. I found that in different countries (e.g., the United States), it is customary that in high schools the teachers have their own classrooms and the students move between the rooms for classes. As a result, there are few cases of teachers being late for their lessons.

I recommend that school administrations throughout the world explore adoption of this approach and set logical lengths of breaks which will make it possible for the students to reach their classes on time and for the teachers to rest a bit between their lessons. This approach will probably decrease the teachers' tardiness, but can also decrease the load and burnout of the teachers, due to their need to run between classrooms. As a result, it might also decrease their voluntary absences due to the desire to regain energy, or their desire to leave the educational system due to the acknowledgment that they belong to an academic profession that requires their own unique physical learning space.

Strategies at the Level of the Departments of Education and Educational Authorities

Strategies Characterized by Care for the Teacher

- *Organization of workshops for teachers at a logical time intervals*: These meetings, especially for the teachers who have been teaching for five years or less (teachers with the high potential for attrition), whichbring together the teachers and the district administration or the administration of an educational network, can give the teachers the feeling that they are important for the system, since senior administration has come to participate. Furthermore, the administration will be aware of the needs that particularly concern young teachers, as well as the needs of the other teachers who participate in these encounters. This interaction can encourage openess between the teachers and the senior administration, and there may also be an increase in level of satisfaction and commitment on the part of the teachers. As a result, the rates of tardiness, absences and attrition will hopefully decrease.

- *Allocation of school mentors*: These mentors will support the needs of all of the teachers, especially those of the new teachers. It is important that the mentors will not be obligated to report to the administration of the department of education or to the educational authority, and they will let the teachers know about this, in order to encourage the teachers to talk to them about their difficulties without fear that they might lose their jobs or professional standing. This activity can contribute to the teachers' desires to continue working in the educational system. This should come to be expressed in lower rates of tardiness to class and an increase in the teachers' presence in school, to the point that few teachers make the decision to leave the system.

Strategies Characterized by Formality toward the Teacher

- *Distribution of a comparative report of rates of tardiness, absences and attrition among teachers in the different schools:* It is important that the school district's administration creates comparative reports on these measures for the school principals. For example, they can create reports that compare schools that belong to the same educational level - elementary school, middle school, high school – or between schools in the same district, or in different districts, or between different schools in an educational network. This report should maintain the anonymity of the schools. For example, there can be a report on teachers' absences that is generated at least twice a year, once at the end of the first semester and once at the end of the second semester. The principals will study the report, and will be encouraged to decrease the teachers' absences during the following years, given the knowledge that this topic is being tracked.

- *Allocation of incentives and grants*: Similar to other groups in the private sector, it is important to award incentives and grants to teachers and schools who have low rate of absence. For example, teachers or a school who have lower absence rates than the national average will receive cash bonuses; a school with a lower level of absence than the district or national average will receive money for social activities for the entire teaching staff of the school. The giving of rewards for not missing school is generally not accepted in the education system, due to the perception that people should not get paid twice for the same activity: salaries for teaching hours and rewards for the teacher's presence in school. Nevertheless, we find that in different organizations, especially in the private sector, grants are given for not missing work, and this facilitates lowering employee absences. Educational systems throughout the world should consider the benefit of giving such a grant since teachers will miss less work days and the school will need to pay out less for sick days.

- *Decrease in teachers' illnesses*: The authorities can develop standards for construction of ventilated classrooms and buildings that are large and sturdy. These standards will help safeguard the teachers' health.

In sum, educational leaders from different educational levels (school principals, superintendents, coordinators, mentors) can use the proposed strategies to lower teachers' withdrawal behaviors by creating an ethical climate that emphasizes the value of caring, and the values of formal and just rules and procedures. These educational leaders can expect both types of ethical climates to increase teachers' commitment and decrease their withdrawal behaviors.

From a practical standpoint, these strategies encourage educational leaders to develop an integrative approach and focus on organizational ethics and sociodemographic predictors in order to reduce teachers' tardiness and absences and to attract high-quality teachers. In particular, educational leaders should promote the development and sustainment of a caring climate that is characterized by procedural justice. They should also reduce tolerating organizational misbehavior in order to reduce teachers' withdrawal behaviors.

More specifically, educational leaders should understand that they have an ethical and moral obligation to create and promote schools that are ethical organizations (Scheurich & Skrla, 2003; Skrla, Scheurich, Garcia, & Nolly, 2004). Such awareness could be achieved through planning and running educational leaders' training programs and workshops which center on ethical education, life stories, and the exploration of diversity issues. Such an approach would help educational leaders understand their ethical and moral duty to create and promote ethics-oriented schools. This can also help them become aware of possible inequities in their schools (Scheurich & Skrla, 2003; Skrla et al., 2004). It is hoped that these educational programs and workshops would help educational leaders not only develop the needed sensitivity concerning issues of need and fairness, but also guide them in how to behave more ethically and effectively. There should be a strong emphasis placed on value-based inspirations, given the great importance that educational institutions assign to personal and organizational values (Starratt, 1991). Therefore, the expectation is that if schools place greater emphasis on ethical standards, this will lead to improved perceptions, attitudes, on the part of the teachers. Furthermore, such an emphasis should also reduce instances and frequencies of withdrawal behaviors.

Section IV

Critical Ethical Incidents in Team-Based Simulations with Educational Leaders

Chapter 25

Critical Ethical Incidents in Educational Leadership

In the following chapters, I present how to assimilate the ethical contents of this book into practice, mainly by using critical ethical incidents and team-based simulations.

The critical incident technique was developed during the Second World War. It grew out of the US Air Force Aviation Psychology Program that was used for selecting and classifying aircrews. Since that time, critical incidents have become a widely used qualitative research method in a number of different disciplines, such as nursing (Kemppainen, 2000), medicine (Butterfield, Borgen, Amundson, & Maglio, 2005), organizational learning (Ellinger & Bostrom, 2002), counseling (Dix & Savickas, 1995), and education and leadership (Le Mare & Sohbat, 2002; Shapira-Lishchinsky, 2014; Tirri & Koro-Ljungberg, 2002).

A critical incident is usually an undesirable situation that an employee experienced (Keatinge, 2002; Rosenal, 1995; Wolf & Zuzelo, 2006) and it refers to an event or situation which served as a significant turning point in the life of a person (Tripp, 2011). In ethical contexts in educational systems, critical ethical incidents are not necessarily sensational events that involve tensions. They may even be minor ethical incidents that happen in every school. Their classification as critical ethical incidents is based on the significance and the meaning the teachers give them (Angelides, 2001).

Critical ethical incidents are important to identify, since they may harm educational leaders' professional development, given that they may lead these leaders to favor one action over another when encountering similar situations (Sikes, Measor, & Woods, 2001). Griffin (2003) studied the effectiveness of using critical ethical incidents in a supervised field experience to develop reflective and critical thinking skills. Her research demonstrated that when the individuals reflected on critical ethical incidents, this increased the orientation toward growth and inquiry.

International Aspects of Organizational Ethics in Educational Systems, 115–116
Copyright © 2018 by Emerald Publishing Limited
All rights of reproduction in any form reserved
doi:10.1108/978-1-78714-777-520181025

Dealing with Ethical Quandaries by Using Critical Ethical Incidents

By encouraging educational leaders to think about critical ethical incidents, we assume that they will know how to deal more successfully with ethical dilemmas in the future (Nilsson, 2009). In another study, Johnson (2003) argued that critical ethical incidents force us to reflect on contradictory values in the school's educational process. Colnerud (1997) proposed that the best way to explore ethical quandaries that educational leaders face is by exploring the critical ethical incidents they deal with in their professional relationships. He used the critical incident technique to examine ethical quandaries that educational leaders face and the conditions that contribute to those quandaries.

Error Management by Critical Ethical Incidents

When people speak about critical ethical incidents and analyze what happened, they can learn from the errors that occurred in a safe and "mistake-forgiving" way, without taking the risk of harming others (e.g., teachers, students, or parents). It has been found that expertise can be improved by learning from errors (Griffin, 2003). At times, educational leaders handle educational mistakes by denial, discounting personal responsibility, and distancing themselves from consequences (Colnerud, 2006; Husu & Tirri, 2003; Thornberg, 2008). When this occurs, critical incident reports can break the code of silence regarding adverse outcomes and mistakes in leadership (Butterfield, Borgen, Amundsen, & Maglio, 2005). Furthermore, from an ethical standpoint, teachers and students have the right to get the best care and support that can be reasonably provided (Tirri & Koro-Ljungberg, 2002). Employing critical ethical incident reports is an excellent way to decrease management errors (Alison & Crego, 2012). Such a method also can convey an ethical message to educational leaders that it is imperative to do the utmost to protect teachers and students whenever possible.

Critical Ethical Incidents for the Promotion of Professional Autonomy

Critical ethical incident reports can stimulate educational leaders' professional autonomy in a number of ways: (1) they promote self-directed professional action; educational leaders develop a solid sense of personal responsibility for their teaching practice by engaging in ongoing reflection (Little, 1995); (2) critical ethical incident reports also advance self-directed professional development. As educational leaders engage in this method, they become aware of how pedagogical skills can be promoted through self-reflection (Smith, 2011); and (3) they enable educational leaders to gain more control over their actions in the educational settings and to experience professional development (Kauffman, Johnson, Kardos, Liu, & Peske, 2002; McGrath, 2000).

When an educational leader has little professional autonomy, this often leads to negative actions and emotions, such as defensiveness, uncertainty, and fear (Ashforth & Lee, 1990). These are not conducive to deal with critical ethical incidents (Clement & Vandenberghe, 2000).

Chapter 26

Team Simulations based on Critical Ethical Incidents among Educational Leaders

For decades, simulation has been used in areas that are outside the educational systems (e.g., the military, medical, legal, and nursing professions) to study concepts in a risk-free training environment (Sugand, Akhtar, Khatri, Cobb, & Gupte, 2015) and to engage in practice of critical thinking skills (Salas, Wildman, & Piccolo, 2009; Weatherspoon, Phillips, & Wyatt, 2015). In addition, team simulations often provide a source of direct intervention that can facilitate leadership and management development through critical ethical incidents (Allen, 2008; Mathieu, Kukenberger, D'innocenzo, & Reilly, 2015). As a rule, simulations comprise a training and feedback method in which participants practice tasks and processes in critical ethical circumstances. They receive immediate and rapid feedback from observers, peers, and video cameras – the simulations are taped – that can help them improve their methods of coping with critical ethical incidents (Moratis, Hoff, & Reul, 2006; Orme & Ashton, 2003).

Research has been conducted on team simulations has found that such work has the potential to increase leadership motivation since participants have the chance to experience situations that reflect reality while testing and investigating "what if" scenarios (Aldrich, 2005; De Freitas & Jarvis, 2007). Studies have also shown that learning activities that re-create leadership situations provide a good learning environment for the transfer of learning (McHugh et al., 2016; Swanson & Holton, 1999). Simulations, which reflect critical ethical incidents, help people who are participating in the simulations to later transfer their knowledge to real educational leadership situations. This is because the simulations provide the participants with opportunities to practice leadership skills in a realistic yet risk-free learning environment (Anderson & Lawton, 2009; Thornton, Mueller-Hanson, & Rupp, 2017).

During team simulations, educational leaders have the opportunity to learn from peer feedback as they engage in their ethical decision-making process, since these leaders participate in role-play that mirrors the functions of decision makers and leaders (Kenworthy & Wong, 2005; Romme, 2004). As a result, this allows the participants to explore different approaches, test diverse strategies, and arrive

International Aspects of Organizational Ethics in Educational Systems, 117–120
Copyright © 2018 by Emerald Publishing Limited
All rights of reproduction in any form reserved
doi:10.1108/978-1-78714-777-520181026

at a better understanding of key and important aspects of the real world (Hill & Semler, 2001; Kenworthy & Wong, 2005; Romme, 2004; Thavikulwat, 2009).

Brookfield's research (1990) found that team simulations, which are based on critical ethical incidents, could promote constructivist learning among educational leaders. The constructivist approach avers that by exposing learners to new experiences, this creates perturbations – forms of mental disquiet that challenge the learner to understand and make sense of new information that results from the new experience (Powell & Kalina, 2009; Shapira-Lishchinsky, 2015).

As a result, team simulations promote constructivist learning by engaging participants' affective and cognitive learning domains. This process often results in a deeper and more memorable experience. In team simulations, leaders engage in role-playing by taking part in active experiential exercises. This has the potential to help participants learn about ethics because the role-play illustrates potential decisions that are to be made in relation to ethical dilemmas (Sims, 2002; Sims & Felton, 2006). The role-playing exercises actively engage educational leaders in the learning process. As Sims (2002) notes, this often leaves a memorable impression on the participants in the simulations.

Nevertheless, there are some barriers to the effectiveness of team simulations. These include participants' perceptions of the learning environment as intimidating or stressful. When participants have these experiences, they cannot only trigger strong emotions but also increase the number of errors that leaders commit, and lead to fear of judgments from colleagues (McGaghie, Issenberg, Petrusa, & Scalese, 2016). There is no doubt that having one's performance analyzed and reflected upon by others, from a critical perspective, can be unnerving (Savoldelli, Naik, Hamstra, & Morgan, 2005). Moreover, real-world situations often differ quite a bit from laboratory-based team simulations in terms of both the intensity of personal involvement in decision-making and the complexity of determinants and outcomes (Lyons et al., 2015; Yusko & Goldstein, 1997).

Educational leadership is perceived by the leaders as a field that offers different ways of situating ethical leadership and addresses blind spots in ethical knowledge and disciplinary ethical practice (Hallinger & Bridges, 2017). Today, interest is focused on the objectives of leadership (example.g., moral and ethical objectives); it does not solely focus on its effects, e.g., goal setting and developing a vision for the school, or creating motivation for achievement (Normore & Brooks, 2014). There has been a growing interest in understanding the managerial processes that promote stability in schools, such as organization and coordination (Brooks & Normore, 2010). Leadership now centers on "moral leadership" and "leadership development," which have received major attention from a number of countries throughout the world (Oplatka, 2009; Oplatka & Addi-Raccah, 2009; Silva et al., 2017). Therefore, there is good reason to use simulations in learning environments that focus on ethical dilemmas in leadership.

Below follow a few examples of team simulations that can be used with educational leaders for the practice of critical ethical incidents.

Example 1

A student who comes from a low-income family in which his parents are divorced is demonstrating problems in a prestigious high school (e.g., he is receiving low marks in his classes, he is often late to class or misses class completely, and he does not submit required homework). His mother has come to you and pleaded that her son be allowed to remain in the school, even if he does not complete the matriculation exams. She wants to prevent him from being "on the street." Your task is to decide the student's future in a team meeting.

The people participating in this meeting are as follows:

(a) The school principal.
(b) The coordinator of the grade-level.
(c) The school counselor.
(d) The student's homeroom teacher.
(e) The student's mother.

Example 2

The students in a certain grade participated in an annual overnight field trip. During the evening, some students become disruptive and broke three doors. The other students do not want to divulge the names of the students who broke the doors.

Your task is to decide whether to continue the trip.

Your team meeting comprised the following members:

(a) The school principal
(b) The school counselor
(c) The homeroom teacher
(d) A student council member

Example 3

Sheila was diagnosed with hyperactivity disorder and prescribed a daily dose of methylphenidate. Her mother refuses to give her daughter this medication, because she has heard that it may have adverse long-term side effects. Meanwhile, Sheila's teachers have been complaining that they are finding it impossible to teach the class with Sheila constantly interrupting.

Your task is to decide whether to let Sheila continue in her class.

The decision will be taken at a team meeting comprisedthe following people:

(a) The school principal
(b) The school counselor
(c) Sheila's homeroom teacher
(d) One of Sheila's parents

Example 4

During recess, in the schoolyard, a teacher found five students smoking marijuana. The students do not want to reveal who brought it and said that their parents bought it and allow them to smoke it.

Your task is to decide how to respond in a team meeting with the following members:

(a) The school principal
(b) The school counselor
(c) The homeroom teacher

Chapter 27

The Gap between Official Educational Policies and Practiced Policies

As presented in Chapter 4, the concept of "morality of justice" is based on attempting to follow universal rules and societal rules (Kohlberg, 1986). Therefore, in this chapter, "morality of justice" will refer to official policy reflected by the law. In cases in which no law is relevant to the ethical case, official policy will include the Ministry of Education's management circulars or school regulations.

The concept "morality of care" reflects a less formal approach by focusing on different aspects of kindness that are distinct from the "morality of justice" in that it does not attempt to follow universal rules. Instead, it focuses on responsiveness to another's needs (Gilligan & Attanucci, 1988). In this chapter, I refer to "morality of care" by focusing on teachers' tendency to act in a caring way. Based on the tension between the "morality of justice" and the "morality of care," it seems that codes of ethics developed by teachers, based on their practice, may help them in their ethical decision making in different national contexts and situations.

In order to offer support to teachers in ethical decision making, different countries (e.g., the United States, Canada, New Zealand) have formulated official policies through state laws and circulars published by educational authorities (O'Neill & Bourke, 2010). However, although the law relates to general topics, such as "human dignity" and "right to freedom," it is often difficult for teachers to decide how to respond to specific critical ethical incidents in practice. Moreover, school life comprises many facets that neither the law nor the educational management circulars have taken into account. Therefore, it seems that teachers could be helped in their day to day ethical decision-making by a code of ethics that clearly spells out desirable behaviors based on their experience.

Previous study (Shapira-Lishchinsky & Gilat, 2015) shows that despite the existence of formal policy (morality of justice) for handling ethical dilemmas, in several cases, the teachers did not know how they were expected to act. The teachers exhibited a tendency to react with empathy and caring (morality of care), even if they were aware that stricter measures were mandated by the law, or in cases in which there was not a law that was relevant for the incident, the educational management circular provided the policy and regulations. A possible explanation

International Aspects of Organizational Ethics in Educational Systems, 121–123
Copyright © 2018 by Emerald Publishing Limited
All rights of reproduction in any form reserved
doi:10.1108/978-1-78714-777-520181027

for this might be that teachers often find it hard to match their tendency to care for their students with some of the state laws required of them.

The study's findings suggest that while teachers are generally expected to care about their educational system, in practice, teachers see themselves as highly committed to caring for their students (morality of care), and it is not uncommon for loyalty to the student to outweigh loyalty to the system. In this study, the tendency to act may diverge from the official policy (morality of justice), which is seen as overly strict and impersonal. Thus, teachers prefer to explore alternative ways to act and demonstrate sensitivity to the student (morality of care).

The discrepancies we noted between teachers' tendency to act and official policy may encourage educational policy to empower the teachers and promote their autonomy to deal with ethical incidents by developing their ethical decision-making process. In this way, teachers will learn how to manage their ethical decision making while balancing between their caring for students and acting according to official policy in a way that will not cause harm to the students or to the educational system. This may be achieved, for example, by team-based simulations, through role modeling the incidents, then investigating the simulations, and finally discussing how to combine legal requirements with teachers' initial tendency to act according to their caring.

In addition, it is not sufficient to formulate official policies (e.g., laws, educational management circular, school rules, or codes of ethics) alone, if our aim is to empower teachers to act in real-life ethical situations. Therefore, educational policy, led by superintendents and school principals, should encourage teachers to develop ethical codes during teachers' professional development programs that may help them in making the future ethical decisions. Although ethical guidelines cannot be formulated to suit every potential ethical dilemma, teachers would be instructed in how to identify instances of conflicting values and how to manage the situation while considering the culture, people, and particular context (Ben-Peretz, 2001).

In any case, despite the desire of many school administrations to create uniform policies and a common language in their schools, there are still discrepancies in the ethical perceptions of the faculty. By encouraging teachers to take part in simulations, and by developing ethical codes during their development programs, we can promote a unified ethical language in schools.

Below are a few examples of scenarios that teachers, in different countries, can practice in workshops, in order to deal with the tensions that exist between official policies and behaviors in practice.

Example 1

One of your secondary school students calls you in the evening, crying, from one of the national parks. Her father beats her, she says, leaving marks on her arms. She asks you to come and see her in the park, but not to tell anybody about it.

Example 2

Several high school students came to school in the evening and wrote graffiti on the walls. The other students did not want to report who wrote the graffiti, although they knew who did it.

Example 3

You are the principal of a private elementary school. The parents do not want a student with special needs to attend the school, even though his parents agree to provide him with an aide. The other parents argue that this is a private school that does not have suitable resources to help students with special needs; therefore, he should attend public school.

Example 4

A secondary school student asks you not to inform her father about her math scores, since she is afraid of his reaction (her parents are divorced). The student's mother supports her request.

Chapter 28

Critical Incidents in Ethical Context: Summary of Updated Studies

In this chapter, I present a summary of several updated studies that explore critical incidents in ethical context.

Developing Authentic Leadership based on Ethical Incidents and Team Simulations

Although there is agreement that authentic leadership should be a necessary element in educational leadership, so far no study has explored whether team-based simulations (TBS) have the potential to promote such leadership. This research (Shapira-Lishchinsky, 2014) aimed to identify whether principal trainees can develop authentic leadership by engaging them in ethical decision making in TBSs of cases they have faced in their work. This study included 50 principal trainees. A four-dimensional model of authentic leadership was constructed that included the following dimensions: balanced processing, internalized moral perspective, relational transparency, and self-awareness. The results demonstrate that leadership programs should include TBSs of ethical incidents, since such simulations can help develop the future authentic leadership of educational leaders.

Learning Ethical Behaviors by Engaging in TBS

This study (Shapira-Lishchinsky, 2013a) explored the learning aspects of TBS by analyzing ethical incidents experienced by 50 students who were under training to become teachers. The results produced a four-dimensional model: (a) learning to arrive at decisions in an environment that was characterized as being "supportive–forgiving"; (b) learning to create standards and principles of care; (c) learning to decrease negative behaviors; and (d) learning to develop an integrative approach in the classroom and schools. Most of the simulations differed from the original incidents. The reason for the differences could be attributed to the fact that the trainees' decision making is highly dependent on the context and the people involved in the event. The results advocate for integrating TBS into the curriculum of teacher training programs.

International Aspects of Organizational Ethics in Educational Systems, 125–126
Copyright © 2018 by Emerald Publishing Limited
All rights of reproduction in any form reserved
doi:10.1108/978-1-78714-777-520181028

Ethical Quandaries in Teachers' Critical Incidents

This research (Shapira-Lishchinsky, 2011), which included 50 teachers, examined ethical dilemmas in critical incidents and the responses that these incidents elicited. As a rule, many teachers prefer to suppress these incidents because they induce unpleasant feelings. By using a grounded theory approach, a three-stage coding process was derived from the data. A multifaceted model of ethical dilemmas emerged from an analysis of 50 critical incidents, which was undertaken using ATLAS.ti 5.0. The classification included the following: (1) a caring climate versus a formal climate; (2) distributive justice versus school standards; (3) confidentiality versus school rules; (4) being loyal to colleagues versus following school norms; and (5) emphasizing the family agenda versus emphasizing educational standards. The results point to the potential of developing educational programs that are based on critical incidents encountered by teachers.

Chapter 29

Scenarios as a Tool for Assimilation of the Book's Contents

One of the common criticisms of academia is that it is disconnected from the field. As a result, this chapter presents additional scenarios for work in simulation groups, which demonstrate the theoretical aspects that have been presented in the book in connection with the training workshops for educational leaders and empowerment of teachers in schools. All the scenarios are presented in the following way: presentation of the case, characteristics of the characters and the event, possible strategies for dealing with the incident, ethical dilemmas, and possible ethical codes derived from the scenario. This format facilitates use of the scenarios by the readers who may want to adopt them for different workshops while developing a strategical approach for different ways of coping with the events.

Case 29.1. Parental Intervention to Remove a Teacher from School

The Case

For over a year, you have been a principal of a challenging elementary school that has a difficult population. The school was close to collapse. You began the job, and have been trying to save the school. The students' parents have no faith in the teachers or in the system. Many have threatened to remove their children. The parents have a great deal of power and influence in the school. The first-grade parents are very dissatisfied with the teacher, and they have demanded that she must not continue with their children in the next year. However, you have no alternative to offer her. You know that the class is extremely difficult and complicated due to the composition of the population in the school and because the teacher did not have any real chance of succeeding. On the other hand, if you do not do what the parents are demanding, many will remove their children from the school and you will have a very big problem.

International Aspects of Organizational Ethics in Educational Systems, 127–138
Copyright © 2018 by Emerald Publishing Limited
All rights of reproduction in any form reserved
doi:10.1108/978-1-78714-777-520181029

Characteristics of the Characters and the Incident

Two parents, who are class representatives, are powerful people. They are assertive, resolute, and determined to have the teacher removed from the school. They set up an emergency meeting at the end of the year (after they attacked the system and personally attacked the teacher throughout the year) and they demand that the principal "get rid" of their children's teacher.

Possible Strategies for Dealing with the Incident ("If–Then")

- If you – the principal – do not adopt the parents' position and support the teacher, the parents will not accept this position. They will talk about you in an aggressive manner and will threaten to take their children out of the school.
- If you, as principal, tell the parents that you will carefully consider their position and weigh the matter, they will say that they heard this in the past and that you are trying to "bide time." Therefore, they will not accept this answer.
- If you examine the problem from the viewpoint of the parents, listen to their difficulties, respond to the difficulties with empathy, and write down what they say, the parents will feel that they have been understood. They will be less aggressive and a bit more willing to listen to your viewpoint.

The Ethical Dilemmas (Possible Ways to Discuss the Event)

- The good of the teacher versus the good of the students.
- Care for the students versus relations with colleagues (principal–teacher).

Possible ethical codes derived from the scenario (possibilities for discussion of the incident)

- I believe that I have to act fairly/justly with the staff of teachers that serve under me. I need to protect them if they have suffered an injustice.

Case 29.2. A Teacher's Determination to Bring about a Change in History Studies

The Case

You are the vice principal of a large middle school. As part of your job, you evaluated a history program because of the complaints made by the students that the lessons were very boring. After your investigation, in which you also compared your school with other schools and consulted with the supervisor, it was decided to change the program in order to increase students' interest in history. As part of the modification, the history books were changed and there was a requirement to alter the content and the order of lessons. Because of these changes, the teachers had to change most of what they had done up to now. The teachers received a detailed announcement about the changes that would be necessary at the beginning of the year, and training sessions with all of the grade-level teachers. At the end of the school year, summation meetings were held individually with each teacher in order to hear what each one had accomplished during the year, how she had incorporated the changes, and what were her recommendations for the coming school year.

The Characteristics of the Characters and the Incident

You, the vice principal of the school, are determined to bring about a change in history studies. One of the history teachers, who has tenure, opposes the change. She has stated that she does not understand at all why a change needs to be made. Up until this year, she taught the old way; student achievements were high; and the students also enjoyed the class. For example, during the entire year, the teacher taught according to the old curriculum and did not change anything.

Possible Strategies for Dealing with the Incident ("If–Then")

- If the vice principal will reprimand the rebellious teacher, the teacher will say that she can propose whatever she wants, but the teachers are the ones authorized in the field. It is the teachers who decide whether to change the learning materials and how to teach the students.
- If the vice principal will respond with wonder at the teacher's assertions, the teacher will say that it only appears to the vice principal that all the teachers are following the orders, but that, in reality, not one of the teachers has actually put the changes into practice, as requested.
- If the vice principal asserts that she knows that the other teachers have integrated the new curriculum into their classes, the teacher will become more entrenched in her position that this is not what happened. In any event, she refuses to teach according to the new program, since almost every year the curriculum is altered and by the time the change hasbeen assimilated, it is changed once again.
- If the vice principal threatens to talk to superiors about the behavior, the teacher will say that she has to make the change, but that she is very uncomfortable with it, and her teaching will reflect this.

The Ethical Dilemmas (Possibilities for Discussion of the Incident)

- Professionalism versus collegial relations.
- The good of the students versus the good of the teachers.

The Ethical Code (Possibilities for Discussion of the Incident)

- I believe that we need to aspire for professionalism in teaching, even at the cost of opposition/resistance from teachers.
- I believe that there is a need to minimize teacher resistance to pedagogical processes that are better for the students.

Case 29.3. A School Principal's Pressure to Raise Student's Grades

The Case

You are a math teacher in a high school in which there are 700 students who come from a middle-high class socioeconomic background. The students, and their parents, think it very important to achieve honors. The parents are highly involved in what happens in the school. They often speak to the teachers and are not afraid to express their positive or negative opinions.

Ron, one of your students in the 11th grade, asked you to raise his grade from 75 to 85 because he thinks he deserves a higher grade. After you turned him down, his mother, who is a central figure on the parents' committee, called the principal and demanded that you raise his grade since the grade you gave him harms Ron, does not reflect his abilities and will ruin his chances to successfully complete his matriculation exams.

The Characteristics of the Characters and the Incident

You are a new teacher; this is your second year in the school. You are admired and have received positive responses from the students and from your colleagues, that is, other teachers. However, you are also aware of the fact that you are just beginning your career; so as a result, you need to continually learn new things, including the way the organization runs, and the curriculum. It is important for you to make a good impression on the people who have influence in the school.

The principal has been in his job for six years. Before that, he was vice principal for many years. He is considered to be honest and task-oriented – a person who thinks that school achievements and the school's good name are very important, especially in comparison to other schools in the region, which are strong competitors.

Possible Strategies for Dealing with the Incident ("If–Then")

- If the principal asserts that the grade does indeed harm the student and does not reflect his knowledge, the teacher will reject the argument and explain that he calculated the grade according to the evaluations that he had and had shown to the students.
- If the principal will say that the parent is highly involved in what happens in the school, always helps and contributes her time, the teacher will explain that, from his point of view, this is not something that needs to be taken into consideration when deciding a student's grade and that he sees this as discriminating against other students.
- If the principal explains that the mother is applying pressure, and has even threatened to go to the supervisor, and as a result, is asking the teacher to reconsider, the teacher will ask for the principal's support.
- If the principal asserts that the teacher still lacks experience in the system, and does not yet understand the powers at work, and as a result, will raise the grade, the teacher will have no choice but to accept the principal's decision.

The Ethical Dilemmas (Possibilities for Discussions on the Incident)

- Collegial relations versus unseemly behavior.
- Equality between students versus parental involvement.

The Derived Ethical Code (Possibilities for Discussion about the Incident)

- I believe that I need to empower the teachers on my staff.
- I believe that I need to serve as a role model for the teachers on my staff.

Case 29.4. Sanctions against Students' Use of Cellphones

The Case

You are the principal of a high school, and as part of your job, you put into practice the decisions made by the Ministry of Education. You announced at the beginning of the school year that, according to the regulations, the teachers are completely forbidden from taking away the students' cellphones – not at the beginning of the class, not in the middle and not at the end. It is also against the rules for the teachers to be responsible for the students' phones. (Last year, your school was forced to pay a large fine for fixing a student's phone that was taken away by the teacher and was accidentally broken, as a result). You asked the grade-level teachers to come up with ways to deal with this problem.

The Characteristics of the Characters and the Incident

The principal is fairly new at her job. Before she was principal, she was a science teacher for many years as well as a homeroom teacher. She is strict about following regulations and procedures in her school, which comprised good students as well as more problematic students, who come from a relatively low socioeconomic status. In addition, she is very strict about following the rules and regulations of the Ministry of Education, and she aspires to meet high standards of student achievement and innovative projects. She employs an "open door policy," in which teachers and students can come to see her in her office whenever they want as long as she is available. When they come, she listens and tries to help.

The teacher is a second-year English teacher (she has been in the system and the school for two years), who teaches each class twice a week for an hour and a half each time. She has completed her student teaching, but had many difficulties during that period, since she didn't always understand how the system works, there were many divisions in the school, and it was very bureaucratic. Moreover, she also had a difficult time with the profession of teaching English. Now, with the beginning of her second year, it is very important to her to succeed and to successfully manage the class, to control what happens in the classroom and to set limits and enforce them.

The young teacher arrives at the principal's office, very distraught. She shares her frustration and helplessness with the principal about the need to deal with the cellphone problem. The students are secretly using their phones during the entire lesson, and not paying attention. In addition to the damage in terms of learning the material, the teacher feels disrespected by the students who use their phones during the lessons, in spite of her requests not to do so.

Possible Strategies for Dealing with the Incident ("If–Then")

- If the teacher is upset, then the principal will try to calm her down and tell her that it is a difficult subject and everyone experiences what she is experiencing. She is not alone.
- If the teachers says that the regulations do not make sense and that the teachers reach a state where there is nothing they can do, then the principal will try, together with her, to find solutions to prevent the frustration.
- If the teacher says that the teachers in the grade level decided on a variety of different rules, and that it is hard for her to enforce the specific regulations in each class, then the principal will ask her to tell her what the different rules are that the grade heads reached. The principal said she would try to come up with a uniform regulation.
- If the teacher says that she is extremely frustrated by the situation, then the principal will ask about other things that are bothering the teacher.

The Ethical Dilemmas (Possibilities for Discussion about the Incident)

- The teacher's status versus maintaining the rules.
- The students' needs versus the teachers' needs.

The Derived Ethical Code (Possibilities for Discussion of the Incident)

- I believe that I need to worry about designing the rules that can actually be applied in the school.
- I believe that I need to support the professional staff when they deal with educational challenges.

Case 5. Dealing with a Student Who Threatened his Teacher

The Case

Daniel, a student of a regular high school located in the geographical periphery, angrily threatened his teacher that he would "slash his tires and burn his car." He yelled and swore, but did not physically approach the teacher. After being suspended for a day, Daniel and his mother were called by the disciplinary committee. He expressed deep remorse for his behavior. The principal needs to decide what to do with the student. Should he allow the student to come back to school under the condition that he begins a special program that tracks and aims to improve Daniel's behavior, or should he tell Daniel to look for another school?

The Characteristics of the Characters and the Incident

Daniel comes from a difficult home; his father does not live with them and he has been in and out of jail over the last few years for different crimes. For the last few years, Daniel has been living with his mother and her partner. During the conversation with the homeroom teacher and with the school counselor, it was learned that just two days before the incident, Daniel's father came to the store where the student works every now and then and bought alcohol and cigarettes on Daniel's account. Daniel's life is very hard now, and it is clear to the principal that no other good school in the area will accept him. If he is forced to leave the school, Daniel will need to find a place in a boarding school for teens, who either drop out of schools or spend their time on the streets.

Possible Strategies for Dealing with the Incident ("If–Then")

- If the principal tells Daniel that he needs to find another school, Daniel will give up and tell everyone at the meeting that if they kick him out of this school, he won't go to school anymore, just to work.
- If the principal decides to let Daniel remain in the school, on condition, then Daniel will say: "It was clear that you would let me stay – you don't really kick out kids from school."
- If the principal turns to Daniel and asks him for his solution, Daniel will lower his head, which shows that he is embarrassed and ask for another chance.

The Ethical Dilemmas (Possibilities for Discussion about the Incident)

- The good of the student versus the good of the school.
- Caring for the student versus caring for the teacher.

The Derived Ethical Code (Possibilities for Discussion about the Incident)

- I believe that I need to worry about the unique needs of my students but not at the expense of hurting others.

Case 29.6. The Unprofessional Teacher

The Case

You are in charge of science studies in a middle school located in the center of the country. The school is considered to be innovative in terms of its pedagogy: there are many training programs for teachers on pedagogical issues. Furthermore, the approach to teaching is one of skill/expertise development, as opposed to "transmission" of knowledge to the students. Nevertheless, the school does not have the optimal means for actually putting the innovative teaching and pedagogical methods into practice.

This year, Meital, a new teacher, joined the science teachers' staff as part of her internship. The science staff comprisedthree science teachers and a coordinator. During the school year, you have noticed that the intern has been performing her tasks in a superficial and partial manner. You called her for a meeting to understand as to what is happening.

Characteristics of the Characters

Meital is a young and new teacher who is interested in expressing herself in the classes she teaches. She became a teacher because she wants to teach and serve as an educational role model for the students. She also loves science. The teacher is idealistic and wants to teach in a different and unique way. She knows about the unique pedagogical approach of the school, but is beginning to lose motivation due to the inability to put the approach into practice. There are also a number of other factors that influence Meital's motivation and desire: the school's bureaucracy, the large number of students in each class (40 per class), and her lack of experience in teaching heterogeneous classrooms (in each class, there are a number of weak students, which fluctuates from class to class), and the large number of classes that she teaches (nine classes).

As a result, opposite is happening now of what she wanted: Meital is only doing the most basic tasks. She is doing the minimum that is required of her. Her lessons became boring. Meital feels that she is not succeeding in managing all the difficulties and tasks, and given that there is no supportive staff, that is, open to her ideas and interested in taking the ideas together with her, she is giving up. As a result, she starts doing the minimum in a superficial manner.

Possible Strategies for Dealing with the Incident ("If–Them")

- If the teacher in charge of science studies asserts that there are many teachers with whom Meital could consult to understand the bureaucracy and succeed in her job, Meital will say that the teachers have not responded nicely to her. Furthermore, they often disparage her ideas and proposals. This lowers her level of motivation.
- If the teacher in charge of science studies asserts that there are tasks that she is required to complete, Meital will say that she does all the tasks assigned to her but it is difficult for her to do work beyond the required tasks. She began the job with a desire to teach, but now she has reached the stage where she is incapable of doing anything more than what she is required to do.
- If the teacher in charge of science studies says that it is the work of a teacher and this is what is expected of her, Meital will say that she isn't sure anymore if this specific school is the right school for her.

Ethical Dilemmas (Possibilities for Discussion about the Incident)

- Caring about the teacher versus caring about meeting school standards.
- Maintaining a teacher versus the welfare of the students.

The Derived Ethical Code (Possibilities for Discussion about the Incident)

- I believe that I must first care about the teacher's professionalism.

Case 29.7. A Teacher's Tardiness to Class

The Case

You are a principal of a middle school, located in the center of the country that has approximately 1,000 students. The school has a good reputation; over the past few years, many students have asked to be accepted into the school and the number of classrooms has considerably grown. About two months after the start of the school year, due to a number of improper student behaviors, the principal said that the policy of acceptance was over for the seventh graders. Since the children were testing the limits, the teachers need to be very strict with them.

The principal emphasized that actually everything begins with the teachers. According to him, there are teachers who think that the bell is not meant for them, and they allow themselves to come into class late. They have been teaching in dirty and messy classes, which make it impossible to get the most out of the class. The principal noted that if a teacher does not get to class on time after a break, then you can't expect the students to arrive on time. Furthermore, there are students who continue to make trouble and there is noise and chaos in their area of the grade.

On the same day, at the end of one of the recesses, the principal saw that Sarah, a teacher, came into class late. He made a comment to her about this and pointed to his watch, in view of the students. Because of the situation, and after thinking about what happened for quite a while, Sarah got up the courage and asked to set up a meeting with the principal, in order to say what she wanted to say.

The Characteristics of the Characters

Sarah, a new math teacher in the school, is a responsible teacher. She invests time in the job and is serious. It is important to note that on the day of the incident, Sarah did not have breaks, since she was on rotation duty. Concerning the incident – Sarah arrived a few minutes late in class since she was coming from her rotation and did not even have time to have water or use the restroom. Sarah was unhappy with the principal's response because he neither asked why she was late and because he noted her tardiness in front of the students. On the other hand, the principal was very angry since in the morning, he had asked all of the teachers not to be late and he had seen Sarah's seventh grade class being wild and waiting for the teacher to open the classroom.

Possible Strategies for Dealing with the Incident ("If–Then")

- If the principal says that it was irresponsible of Sarah to get to class late, especially since he had spoken about this to all of the grade-level teachers, then Sarah will respond that it was only a few minutes, that she had just finished her rotation duties, and had not even managed to get a drink of water. She will emphasize that she is a responsible and punctual teacher and that she was never late to class before. Furthermore, it was unseemly to reprimand her in front of the students.

- If the principal will explain why it is important not to be tardy, and the consequences of being late, then Sarah will say that she agrees with him. However, in this case, it was unavoidable.
- If the principal will say that he misinterpreted the situation and that he apologizes for how he handled things, Sarah will emphasize that she was hurt by his response and that she does not think that she deserved such a response; it is always important to first examine the reasons for what has happened.

The Ethical Dilemmas (Possibilities for Discussion about the Incident)

- Maintaining rules/regulations versus care for the teacher.
- Concern for the teacher versus concern for the students.

The Derived Ethical Code (Possibilities for Discussion about the Incident)

- I believe that I must carefully examine each case before reprimanding a teacher.
- I believe that my behavior needs to be respectful toward the teachers on my staff.

Case 29.8. Keeping New Teachers in the System

The Case

For six years, you have been a principal of a school with 850 students. The school takes in many students from different sectors. Some of them live in the boarding-school on the campus. The 10th grade has five classes – three have students with medium to high abilities and two have students with low learning abilities. As the school principal, you are responsible for creating the schedule, bringing in new teachers, and helping them successfully integrate into the system.

Anat is a new teacher who teaches English to the 10th grade, which has students with low learning abilities. She asks to meet with you three months after the beginning of the school year along with a teacher who is helping her integrate into the system. She wants to speak to you about the difficulty in coping with classes such as these, without prior teaching experience. She wants to stress upon the difficulty, since these classes also have large numbers of students, many disciplinary problems, and a lack of teachers' aides that were promised when she accepted the position.

The Characteristics of the Characters

Anat completed her undergraduate degree in English with honors and worked in the Ministry of Foreign Affairs for five years. Due to her personal and social-based ideology, which is important to have an impact on the educational system,

Anat chose to take a job in a project that recruits graduates with honors and integrates them into the educational system in jobs in which leadership is needed, as well as social responsibility. She is very happy that she was accepted into a school which has high social values and that integrates boarding school children who are in need of extra educational–social help.

When Anat met her mentor teacher, she was told that the classes that she would teach would comprise 10 students each with low learning abilities. Moreover, the mentor promised her that a teacher's aide would work with her and that she would take part in training sessions given by the professional school staff.

Three months later, Anat is very frustrated; the disciplinary problems are very difficult and getting worse, the number of students is much larger than what she was promised, and there is no teaching aide. In order to deal with the situation, Anat works for long hours at home to prepare and grade the papers. She makes many phone calls to the parents and is compiling a class schedule. This is the background to Anat's request to meet with the principal and the mentor. She feels that the school is not providing her with the needed and significant support and training. She also feels that the school is making a mistake by placing inexperienced teachers in the most difficult and challenging classes, and that this is not what the school administration promised her.

Possible Strategies for Dealing with the Situation ("If–Then")

- If the principal will say that the school does not have the budget to provide a teacher's aide or to decrease the number of students in the class, the teacher will say that as part of her work contract, she was promised to teach small classes and receive help from the school staff. Therefore, there is a breach of contract. In addition, for the 11th grade, the English teachers have teachers' aides and this has a direct impact on the atmosphere in the class, as well as on the achievements of the students. The school needs to ensure the success of all of the students and to strengthen and support the new teachers in order to ease their integration into the school.
- If the principal says that the teacher needs to be more assertive and exhibit a higher level of leadership in the classroom, by taking care of the disciplinary problems by herself, and that there is no possibility of putting her into other classes due to needs of the system, the teacher will say that the school, as an institution that hires new teachers, needs to offer pre-training in order to give the new teachers practical tools and solutions to handle important topics, such as problems of violence and lack of motivation on the part of the students. It is unfair to place the burden of teaching large classes that have significantly more problems than the other classes, on the new teacher, who has no prior teaching experience. She is very unhappy because she does not yet have the suitable/relevant tools to cope with such challenging classes. It is her perception that the senior teachers have no interest in teaching such difficult classes and, as a result, they gave her these classes, since they know that as a new teacher, it will be difficult for her to refuse.

- If the principal says that she understands that it is hard for the teacher who is just beginning her teaching career, and that this is a big burden but she needs to feel encouraged and feel satisfaction from the students' small successes, then the teacher needs to voice her personal feeling that she does not feel that she has an educational staff that is supporting and helping her along the way. She feels that she is expected to deal with the problems on her own. She has to deal all alone, with the challenging students and with the school bureaucracy. This gives her the feeling that perhaps she made a mistake in moving over to the teaching profession and that she is not succeeding in integrating, as she had hoped.

The Ethical Dilemmas (Possibilities for Discussion of the Incident)

- Keeping new teachers versus the needs of the system.
- The teacher's welfare versus the limit of school resources.

The Derived Ethical Code (Possibilities for Discussion of the Incident)

- I believe that I need to empower and support the new generation of teachers in educational system.
- I believe that I have to worry about the professional welfare of teachers.

Chapter 30

Summary and Conclusions

This book was unique in that it took an organizational approach to the understanding of the concept of ethics in educational systems, as well as having a global orientation to this concept. To date, there have been very few studies in the field of educational administration that have dealt with the concept of ethics, using this approach.

The book makes it possible for researchers, educators, and teachers, holding different positions throughout the world, such as educational leaders and administrators, as well as personnel who are at the pedagogical forefront (supervisors, school principals, teachers, pedagogical heads, and educational counselors), to understand what they need to do in order to advance the ethical culture in educational systems. This book emphasizes that to advance this culture, it is important to encourage the involvement of the schools, parents, and community, and to work for the strengthening of collegial relationships among teachers. It encourages the professional development of teachers, not only on the learning level, but also by helping them gain awareness that the educator, regardless of his/her position and responsibilities, serves as a role model both inside and outside the educational system. Furthermore, the book stressed on the importance of additional structural dimensions, such as concern for the student and the safeguarding and maintaining of rules and regulations.

The book can further help educational leaders understand the complexity of their roles in relation to organizational ethics via the multi-dimensional model of the different ethical dilemmas they face, including dilemmas such as: the school's educational agenda vs. the family's educational agenda; teachers' autonomy vs. school interests; the promotion of egalitarianism among students vs. attending to differential students' needs; and concern for the teacher vs. caring for the students. This will allow them to develop a systemic approach to coping with ethical challenges in educational organizations.

This book offered different aspects of the meaning of organizational ethics by focusing on international aspects. It begins with a description of the international aspects by considering the development of ethical codes as instruments that can minimize teachers' inappropriate behaviors, including withdrawal behaviors, by

International Aspects of Organizational Ethics in Educational Systems, 139–141
Copyright © 2018 by Emerald Publishing Limited
All rights of reproduction in any form reserved
doi:10.1108/978-1-78714-777-520181030

describing processes that occur in different educational systems in the world and the contribution of ethical codes to quality education and professional empowerment. Moreover, the book deals with organizational ethics from the viewpoint of educational leadership that finds expression in ethical decision-making.

The book then focused on the relationship between perceptions of organizational ethics and teachers' withdrawal behaviors that concern human resources management. The book avers that there is a transition to withdrawal behaviors, which cannot be prevented due to constraints, such as illness, family bereavement and other unfortunate events, and/or when teachers perceive different factors in the educational system as treating them in an unjust manner. As a result, teachers, at times, will respond with behaviors that are perceived as being unethical. I am careful to note that, at times, these are over-simplified perceptions which do not take into account unusual cases in which withdrawal makes it possible for the teacher to later return to the classroom with renewed energies. As a result, these behaviors can increase the teacher's effectiveness.

Furthermore, the book presents cases in which the schools' regulations or the policy of the educational headquarters in different countries compel the teachers at times to lie and withdraw from their work due to inflexibility and inconsideration of the teachers' unique needs. Moreover, the book presents an approach that asserts that at times there is a discrepancy between the level of the manifest policy and what happens on the ground due to the inflexibility of the system concerning teachers' perceptions and beliefs.

The book also shows that at times the withdrawal behaviors are voluntary due to the perceptions concerning organizational ethics. Teachers' withdrawal behaviors such as tardiness, absenteeism, and attrition are found in many educational systems throughout the world. Human resources' administrations in educational organizations face challenges when attempting to decrease these phenomena, since such behaviors cause numerous economic loss and harm the effectiveness of learning. The uniqueness of this book is that it examined teachers' withdrawal behaviors from a different aspect by looking at the phenomena through perceptions of organizational ethics and their relationships with these behaviors. The book avers that in spite of the fact that lateness, absences, and attrition are categorized under the term "withdrawal behaviors," and are responses to perceptions of low organizational ethics in schools, it is important to differentiate between them and to work in different ways to minimize their appearance on the individual, school, national, and even international levels by undertaking international evaluations.

In order to offer a systemic viewpoint, the book presented an integrative moderating model in which organizational commitment moderates perceptions of organizational ethics (the type of ethical climate, organizational justice, the tendency to misbehave, and the psychological contract) and withdrawal behaviors (including tardiness, absenteeism, and attrition). Furthermore, the model also incorporates the traditional variables that have been researched in the past when attempting to predict teachers' withdrawal behaviors, such as personal characteristics (gender, age, seniority, and the role in school) and organizational characteristics (school size, school regulations, and procedures).

In order to complete the systemic perspective, the book describes the behaviors perceived as being the opposite of withdrawal behaviors – organizational citizenship behaviors. The book showed that approaching these two types of behavior as being mere opposites of one another is too simplistic, since recent findings have shown that educators and teachers can simultaneously engage in both voluntary withdrawal and citizenship behaviors due to positive motivations, such as the desire to take care of pressing disciplinary problems which keep the teacher from reaching her classroom on time. Moreover, the book presented recent studies that focus on the relationships between organizational ethical perceptions and teachers' withdrawal behaviors. It offered a variety of critical ethical events that highlight teachers' withdrawal behaviors that can be used for discussion, learning and training for effectively dealing with teachers' withdrawal behaviors.

This section of the book ended with a number of strategies for minimizing withdrawal behaviors, which can be integrated into work. Some of them are on the school level and some are on the level of the headquarters of the ministries of education found throughout the world. There was a focus on the strategy of caring versus strategies that focus on formal arrangements. As a result, the approach taken in this book was that there is a need to work in a sensitive and committed manner in order to decrease withdrawal behaviors.

The last section of the book offers suggestions for different trainings and workshops, which are based on analyses of critical ethical events and group simulations for the promotion of ethics in the school. An emphasis was placed on the way the principals cope/deal with these challenges when they interact with students, teachers, supervisors and parents. The simulations are constructed in a way that makes it possible to practice them in training sessions for teachers and principals and in schools' continuing education courses for teachers. They employ techniques for developing strategy skills, which give participants the opportunity to respond to a number of different scenarios.

I believe that the book can contribute to all people engaged in academic research in educational work – teachers, principals, supervisors, heads of educational departments in educational authorities, and administrative managers. It can help the personnel understand the factors behind teachers' withdrawal behaviors and the consequences of these behaviors. This understanding can encourage the creation of a policy of intervention which can improve the ethical culture and climate in schools, as well as the justice in the schools. Such an improvement can help minimize teachers' withdrawal behaviors.

References

Abdolmohammadi, M. J., Read, W. J., & Scarbrough, D. P. (2003). Does selection-socialization help to explain accountants' weak ethical reasoning? *Journal of Business Ethics*, *42*(1), 71–81.

Adams, J. S. (1965). Inequity in social exchange. In L. Berkowitz (Ed.), *Advances in experimental social psychology* (Vol. 2, pp. 267–299). New York, NY: Academic Press.

Adams, P. (2015). In defence of care: Gilligan's relevance for primary education. *Pedagogy, Culture & Society*, *23*(2), 281–300. doi:10.1080/14681366.2014.994662

Addae, H. M., Johns, G. J., & Boies, K. (2013). The legitimacy of absenteeism *from* work: A nine-nation exploratory study. *Cross-Cultural Management*, *20*(3), 402–428.

Addi-Raccah, A., & Ainhoren, R. (2009). School governance and teachers' attitudes to parents' involvement in schools. *Teaching and Teacher Education*, *25*(6), 805–813.

Ajzen, I. (2012). The theory of planned behavior. In P. A. M. Lange, A. W. Kruglanski, & E. T. Higgins (Eds.), *Handbook of theories of social psychology* (Vol. 1, pp. 438–459). London: SAGE.

Ajzen, I., & Fishbein, M. (2005). The influence of attitudes on behavior. In D. Albarracín, B. T. Johnson, & M. P. Zanna (Eds.), *The handbook of attitudes* (pp. 173–221). Mahwah, NJ: Erlbaum.

Alcázar, L., Rogers, F. H., Chaudhury, N., Hammer, J., Kremer, M., & Muralidharan, K. (2006). Why are teachers absent? Probing service delivery in Peruvian primary schools. *International Journal of Educational Research*, *45*(3), 117–136.

Alcover, C. M., Rico, R., Turnley, W. H., & Bolino, M. C. (2017). Understanding the changing nature of psychological contracts in 21st century organizations: A multiple-foci exchange relationships approach and proposed framework. *Organizational Psychology Review*, *7*(1), 4–35.

Aldrich, C. (2005). *Learning by doing*. San Francisco, CA: Pfeiffer.

Alison, L., & Crego, J. (Eds.). (2012). *Policing critical incidents: Leadership and critical incident management*. New York, NY: Routledge.

Allen, S. J. (2008). Simulations as a source of learning: Using Star Power to teach ethical leadership and management. *Journal of Leadership Education*, *7*(1), 140–148.

Allisey, A., Rodwell, J., & Noblet, A. (2016). An application of an extended effort-reward imbalance model to police absenteeism behaviour. *Personnel Review*, *45*(4), 663–680.

Altinkurt, Y., Yilmaz, K., & Karaman, G. (2015). The effect of gender, seniority and subject matter on the perceptions of organizational justice of teachers: A meta-analytical study. *Educational Sciences: Theory and Practice*, *15*(1), 33–43.

Anderson, P. H., & Lawton, L. (2009). Business simulations and cognitive learning: Developments, desires, and future directions. *Simulation & Gaming*, *40*(2), 193–216.

Angelides, P. (2001). The development of an efficient technique for colleting and analyzing qualitative data. The analysis of critical incidents. *International Journal of Qualitative Studies in Education*, *14*(3), 429–442.

Appelbaum, S. H., Iaconi, G. D., & Matousek, A. (2007). Positive and negative deviant workplace behaviors: Causes, impacts, and solutions. *Corporate Governance: The International Journal of Business in Society*, *7*(5), 586–598.

Apple, M. W., Au, W., & Gandin, L. A. (Eds.). (2011). *The Routledge international handbook of critical education*. New York, NY: Taylor & Francis.

Arshad, R. (2016). Psychological contract violation and turnover intention: Do cultural values matter? *Journal of Managerial Psychology*, *31*(1), 251–264.

Ashforth, B. E., & Lee, R. T. (1990). Defensive behavior in organizations: A preliminary model. *Human Relations, 43*(7), 621–648.

Aslan, M., & Bakir, A. A. (2017). Evaluation of prospective teachers in terms of academic self-efficacy and professional competence. *European Journal of Educational Research, 6*(4), 553–563.

Astin, A. W., & Astin, H. S. (2000). Leadership reconsidered: Engaging higher education in social change. Retrieved from http://www.wkkf.org/Pubs/CCT/ Leadership/Pub3368. PDF

Avolio, B. J. (2007). Promoting more integrative strategies for leadership theory building. *American Psychologist, 62*(1), 25–33.

Baete, G. S. (2011). Differentiating school leadership: Facing the challenges of practice. *School Leadership & Management, 31*(5), 545–548.

Bal, P. M., de Lange, A.H., Ybema, J. F., Mandy, E. G., Jansen, P.G. W., & van der Velde, M. E. G. (2011). Age and trust as moderators in the relation between procedural justice and turnover: A large-scale longitudinal study. Applied Psychology: *An International Review, 60*(1), 66–86. doi: 10.1111/j.1464-0597.2010.00427.x

Balow, H. C. (2015). *Multiple predictors of tardiness behavior.* Beaumont, TX: Lamar University-Beaumont.

Bandura, A. (1977). Self-efficacy: Toward a unifying theory of behavioral change. *Psychological Review, 84*(2), 191.

Banks, J. A. (2015). *Cultural diversity and education. Foundations, curriculum and teaching (5th ed.).* Boston, MA: Pearson.

Begley, A. M. (2003). Creative approaches to ethics: Poetry, prose and dialogue. In V. Tschuding (Ed.), *Approaches to ethics: Nursing beyond boundaries* (pp. 125–136). London: Butterworth-Heinemann.

Begley, P. T. (2001). In pursuit of authentic school leadership practices. *International Journal of Leadership in Education, 4*(4), 353–366.

Begley, P. T. (2006). Self-knowledge, capacity and sensitivity: Prerequisites to authentic leadership by school principals. *Journal of Educational Administration, 44*(6), 570–589.

Begley, P. T., & Johansson, O. (Eds.). (2006). *The ethical dimensions of school leadership* (Vol. 1). Amsterdam, the Netherlands: Springer Science & Business Media.

Begley, P. T., & Stefkovich, J. (2007). Integrating values and ethics into postsecondary teaching for leadership development: Principles, concepts, and strategies. *Journal of Educational Administration, 45*(4), 398–412.

Ben Peretz, M. (2001). The impossible role of teacher educators in a changing world. *Journal of Teacher Education, 52*(1), 48–56.

Ben Sasson, D., & Somech, A. (2015). Observing aggression of teachers in school teams. *Teachers and Teaching, 21*(8), 941–957.

Benito, R., Alegre, M. À., & Gonzàlez-Balletbò, I. (2014). School segregation and its effects on educational equality and efficiency in 16 OECD comprehensive school systems. *Comparative Education Review, 58*(1), 104–134.

Bennett, R., & Stamper, C. L. (2001). Corporate citizenship and deviancy: A study of discretionary work behavior. In C. S. Galbraith & C. H. Stiles (Eds.), *Strategies and organizations in transition* (pp. 265–284). Bingley: Emerald.

Benson, P. G., & Pond, S. B. (1987). An investigation of the process of employee withdrawal. *Journal of Business and Psychology, 1*(3), 218–229.

Berg, J. K., & Cornell, D. (2016). Authoritative school climate, aggression toward teachers, and teacher distress in middle school. *School Psychology Quarterly, 31*(1), 122–136.

Bird, J. J., & Wang, C. (2011). Authentic leadership and budget-building: Superintendents reveal origins, strategies, and connections. *Academy of Educational Leadership Journal, 15*(3), 143–160.

Blau, G. (2002). New conceptualizations of lateness since Blau, 1994. In M. Koslowsky & M. Krausz (Eds.), *Voluntary employee withdrawal and in attendance* (pp. 161–165). New York, NY: Springer.

Blau, G., Surges Tatum, D., & Ward Cook, K. (2004). Comparing correlates for different types of absence versus lateness behaviors. *Journal of Allied Health, 33*(4), 238–246.

Bogotch, I. E. (2000, November). Educational leadership and social justice: Theory into practice. Revised Version of a Paper presented at the Annual Conference of the University Council for Educational Administration, Albuquerque, NM. ERIC Document Reproduction Service No. ED 452–585.

Bok, S. (2002). *Common values*. Columbia, MO: University of Missouri Press.

Bouhlila, D. S. (2015). The Heyneman–Loxley effect revisited in the Middle East and North Africa: Analysis using TIMSS 2007 database. *International Journal of Educational Development, 42*, 85–95.

Bowers, C. A. (2001). *Educating for eco-justice and community*. Athens, GA: University of Georgia Press.

Bowers, T., & McIver, M. (2000). *Ill health retirement and absenteeism amongst teachers*. London: Department of Education and Employment.

Boylan, M., & Woolsey, I. (2015). Teacher education for social justice: Mapping identity spaces. *Teaching and Teacher Education, 46*, 62–71.

Branson, C. M., & Gross, S. J. (Eds.). (2014). *Handbook of ethical educational leadership*. New York, NY: Routledge.

Brault, M. C., Janosz, M., & Archambault, I. (2014). Effects of school composition and school climate on teacher expectations of students: A multilevel analysis. *Teaching and Teacher Education, 44*, 148–159.

Braun, A. (2015). The politics of teaching as an occupation in the professional borderlands: The interplay of gender, class and professional status in a biographical study of trainee teachers in England. *Journal of Education Policy, 30*(2), 258–274.

Brennan, J., Patel, K., & Tang, W. (2009). *Diversity in the student learning experience and time devoted to study: A comparative analysis of the UK and European evidence: Report to HEFCE by the Centre for Higher Education Research and Information*. London: Centre for Higher Education Research and Information, The Open University.

Brookfield, S. (1990). Using critical incidents to explore learners' assumptions. In J. Meziro (Ed.), *Fostering critical reflection in adulthood: A guide to transformative and emancipatory learning* (pp. 177–193), San Francisco, CA: Jossey Bass.

Brooks, J. S., & Normore, A. H. (2010). Educational leadership and globalization: Literacy for a global perspective. *Educational Policy, 24*(1), 52–82.

Brown, M. E., Trevinob, L. K., & Harrison, D. A. (2005). Ethical leadership: A social learning perspective for construct development and testing. *Organizational Behavior and Human Decision Processes, 97*(2), 117–134.

Bullough, R. V. (2011). Ethical and moral matters in teaching and teacher education. *Teaching and Teacher Education, 27*(1), 21–28.

Burke, R. J., Tomlinson, E. C., & Cooper, C. L. (2016). *Crime and corruption in organizations: Why it occurs and what to do about it*. New York, NY: Routledge.

Burton, J. P., Lee, T. W., & Holtom, B. C. (2002). The influence of motivation to attend, ability to attend, and organizational commitment on different types of absence behaviors. *Journal of Management Issues, 14*(2), 181–197.

Butterfield, L. D., Borgen, W. A., Amundson, N. E., & Maglio, A. S. T. (2005). Fifty years of the critical incident technique: 1954–2004 and beyond. *Qualitative Research, 5*(4), 475–497.

Camden, M. C., Price, V. C., & Ludwig, T. D. (2011). Reducing absenteeism and rescheduling among grocery store employees with point-contingent rewards. *Journal of Organizational Behavior Management, 31*(2), 140–149.

Cameron, K. S., & Quinn, R. E. (2011). *Diagnosing and changing organizational culture: Based on the competing values framework*. San Francisco, CA: John Wiley.

Cameron, R. A., & O'Leary, C. (2015). Improving ethical attitudes or simply teaching ethical codes? The reality of accounting ethics education. *Accounting Education, 24*(4), 275–290.

Campbell, E. (2000). Professional ethics in teaching: Towards the development of a code of practice. *Cambridge Journal of Education, 30*(2), 203–221.

Campbell, H. (2012). Planning to change the world: Between knowledge and action lies synthesis. *Journal of Planning Education and Research, 32*(2), 135–146.

Carasco, E. F., & Singh, J. B. (2003). The content and focus of the codes of ethics of the world's largest transnational corporations. *Business and Society Review, 108*(1), 71–94. https://doi.org/10.1111/1467-8594.00007

Carlsen, B. (2012). From absence to absenteeism? A qualitative cross case study of teachers' views on sickness absence. *The Journal of Socio-Economics, 41*, 129–136.

Carpenter, N. C., & Berry, C. M. (2017). Are counterproductive work behavior and withdrawal empirically distinct? A meta-analytic investigation. *Journal of Management, 43*(3), 834–863.

Carr, D. (2005). *Professionalism and ethics in teaching* (Vol. 2). New York, NY: Routledge.

Casimir, G., Ngee Keith Ng, Y., Yuan Wang, K, & Ooi, G. (2014). The relationships amongst leader–member exchange, perceived organizational support, affective commitment, and in-role performance: A social-exchange perspective. *Leadership & Organization Development Journal, 35*(5), 366–385.

Castro, M., Expósito-Casas, E., López-Martín, E., Lizasoain, L., Navarro-Asencio, E., & Gaviria, J. L. (2015). Parental involvement on student academic achievement: A meta-analysis. *Educational Research Review, 14*, 33–46.

Chen, C. C., Chen, M. Y. C., & Liu, Y. C. (2013). Negative affectivity and workplace deviance: The moderating role of ethical climate. *The International Journal of Human Resource Management, 24*(15), 2894–2910.

Chockalingam, V., & Deniz, S. O. (2002). Examining the construct of organizational justice: A meta-analytic evaluation of relations with work attitudes and behaviors. *Journal of Business Ethics, 38*(3), 193–203.

Choi, D., Oh, I. S., & Colbert, A. E. (2015). Understanding organizational commitment: A meta-analytic examination of the roles of the five-factor model of personality and culture. *Journal of Applied Psychology, 100*(5), 1542–1567.

Christians, C. G., Fackler, M., Richardson, K. B., Kreshel, P. J., & Woods, R.H. (2015). *Media ethics: Cases and moral reasoning* (9th ed.) New York, NY: Routledge.

Clandinin, D. J., Long, J., Schaefer, L., Downey, C. A., Steeves, P., Pinnegar, E., & Wnuk, S. (2015). Early career teacher attrition: Intentions of teachers beginning. *Teaching Education, 26*(1), 1–16.

Clinton, M. E., & Guest, D. E. (2014). Psychological contract breach and voluntary turnover: Testing a multiple mediation model. *Journal of Occupational and Organizational Psychology, 87*(1), 200–207.

Cochran-Smith, M. (2009). Toward a theory of teacher education for social justice. Part 2. In A. Hargreaves, A. Lieberman, M. Fullan, & D. Hopkins (Eds.), *Second international handbook of educational change* (pp. 445–467). New York, NY: Springer.

Cohen, A. (2003). *Multiple commitments in the workplace: An integrative approach*. New York, NY: Psychology Press.

Cohen, A. (2014). Organizational commitment research: Past, present and future. In Z. Zhao & F. Rauner (Eds.), *Areas of vocational education research* (pp. 261–274). Berlin, Germany: Springer.

Cohen, A. (2015). *Fairness in the workplace*. London: Palgrave Macmillan.

Coleman, J. S., Campbell, E. Q., Hobson, C. J., McPartland, J., Mood, A. M., Weinfeld, F. D., & York, R. L. (1966). *Equality of educational opportunity*. Washington, DC: Congressional Printing Office.

Collier, L. (2011). The need for teacher communities: An interview with Linda Darling-Hammond. *Council Chronicle: The National Council of Teachers of English, 21*(2), 12–14.

Collins, M. D., Jackson, C. J., Walker, B. R., O'Connor, P. J., & Gardiner, E. (2017). Integrating the context-appropriate balanced attention model and reinforcement sensitivity theory: Towards a domain-general personality process model. *Psychological Bulletin, 143*(1), 91.

Colnerud, G. (1997). Ethical dilemmas of psychologists: A Swedish example in an international perspective. *European Psychologist, 2*(2), 164–170. http://dx.doi.org/10.1027/1016-9040.2.2.164

Colnerud, G. (2006). Teacher ethics as a research problem: Syntheses achieved and new issues. *Teachers and Teaching: Theory and Practice, 12*(3), 365–385.

Colquitt, J. A., LePine, J. A., Piccolo, R. F., Zapata, C. P., & Rich, B. L. (2012). Explaining the justice-performance relationship: Trust as exchange deepener or trust as uncertainty reducer? *Journal of Applied Psychology, 97*(1), 1–23.

Cullen, J. B., Parboteeah, K. P., & Victor, B. (2004). The effects of ethical climates on organizational commitment: A two-study analysis. *Journal of Business Ethics, 46*(2), 127–141.

Cullen, J. B., K. Parboteeah, K., & Victor, B. (2003). The effects of ethical climates on organizational commitment: A two-study analysis *Journal of Business Ethics, 46,* 127–141.

Cullen, J. B., Victor, B., & Bronson, J. W. (1993). The ethical climate questionnaire: An assessment of its development and validity. *Psychological Reports, 73*(2), 667–674.

Dalal, R. S. (2005). A meta-analysis of the relationship between organizational citizenship behavior and counterproductive work behavior. *Journal of Applied Psychology, 90,* 1241–1255.

Dalgleish, T., & Power, M. (Eds.). (2000). *Handbook of cognition and emotion.* New York, NY: John Wiley.

Darling-Hammond, L. (2017). Teacher education around the world: What can we learn from international practice? *European Journal of Teacher Education, 40*(3), 291–309.

Davis, S., Darling-Hammond, L., LaPointe, M., & Meyerson, D. (2005). *School leadership study: Developing successful principals.* Stanford, CA: Stanford Educational Leadership Institute.

DeAngelis, K. J., Wall, A. F., & Che, J. (2013). The impact of preservice preparation and early career support on novice teachers' career intentions and decisions. *Journal of Teacher Education, 64*(4), 338–355.

De Freitas, S., & Jarvis, S. (2007). Serious games-engaging training solutions: A research and development project for supporting training needs. *British Journal of Educational Technology, 38*(3), 523–525.

Deery, S., Walsh, J., & Zatzick, C. D. (2014). A moderated mediation analysis of job demands, presenteeism, and absenteeism. *Journal of Occupational and Organizational Psychology, 87*(2), 352–369.

Delp, S. C. (2014). The high school principal's influence on novice teacher induction within a distributed leadership framework. *Journal of School Public Relations, 35*(2), 132–157.

Denison, D. R. (1996). What is the difference between organizational culture and organizational climate? A native's point of view on a decade of paradigm wars. *Academy of Management Review, 21*(3), 619–654.

Derycke, H., Vlerick, P., Van de Ven, B., Rots, I., & Clays, E. (2013). The impact of effort-reward imbalance and learning motivation on teachers' sickness absence. *Stress and Health, 29*(1), 14–21.

Dewey, J. (2007). *Democracy and education.* Whitefish, MT: Kessinger.

Dineen, B. R., Lewicki, R. J., & Tomlinson, E. C. (2006). Supervisory guidance and behavioral integrity: Relationships with employee citizenship and deviant behavior. *Journal of Applied Psychology, 91*(3), 622.

DiPaola, M., & Tschannen-Moran, M. (2014). Organizational citizenship behavior in schools and its relationship to school climate. *Journal of School Leadership, 11*(5), 424–447.

Dishon-Berkovits, M., & Koslowsky, M. (2002). Determinants of employee punctuality. *The Journal of Social Psychology, 142*(6), 723–739.

Dix, J. E., & Savickas, M. L. (1995). Establishing a career: Developmental tasks and coping responses. *Journal of Vocational Behavior, 47*(1), 93–107.

Donnelly, J. (2013). *Universal human rights in theory and practice* (2nd ed.). Ithaca, NY and London, UK: Cornell University Press.

Doppenberg, J. J., Bakx, A. W. E. A., & Brok, P. J. d. (2012). Collaborative teacher learning in different primary school settings. *Teachers and Teaching, 18*(5), 547–566.

Dover, A. G. (2013). Teaching for social justice: From conceptual frameworks to classroom practices. *Multicultural Perspectives, 15*(1), 3–11.

Duflo, E., Hanna, R., & Ryan, S. P. (2012). Incentives work: Getting teachers to come to school. *American Economic Review, 102*(4), 1241–1278.

Duignan, P. (2014). Authenticity in educational leadership: History, ideal, reality. *Journal of Educational Administration, 52*(2), 152–172.

Duncan-Andrade, J. M. R., & Morrell, E. (2008). *The art of critical pedagogy: Possibilities for moving from theory to practice in urban schools.* New York, NY: Peter Lang.

Edralin, D. M. (2015). Why do workers misbehave in the workplace? *Journal of Management, 2*(1), 88–108.

Edwards, A. P., & Shepherd, G. J. (2007). An investigation of the relationship between implicit personal theories of communication and community behavior. *Communication Studies, 58*(4), 359–375.

Ehrich, L. C., Kimber, M., Millwater, J., & Cranston, N. (2011). Ethical dilemmas: A model to understand teacher practice. *Teachers and Teaching: Theory and Practice, 17*(2), 173–185.

Ejere, E. I. (2010). Absence from work: A study of teacher absenteeism in selected public primary schools in Uyo, Nigeria. *International Journal of Business and Management, 5*(9), 115–128.

Ellinger, A. D., & Bostrom, R. P. (2002). An examination of managers' beliefs about their roles as facilitators of learning. *Management Learning, 33*(2), 147–179.

Eyal, O., Berkovich, I., & Schwartz, T. (2011). Making the right choices: Ethical judgments among educational leaders. *Journal of Educational Administration, 49*(4), 396–413.

Forsyth, D. R., O'Boyle Jr., E. H., & McDaniel, M. A. (2008). East meets West: A meta-analytic investigation of cultural variations in idealism and relativism. *Journal of Business Ethics, 83*, 813–833.

Foust, M. S., Elicker, J. D., & Levy, P. E. (2006). Development and validation of a measure of an individual's lateness attitude. *Journal of Vocational Behavior, 69*(1), 119–133.

Fox, S., Spector, P. E., & Miles, D. (2001). Counterproductive work behavior (CWB) in response to job stressors and organizational justice: Some mediator and moderator tests for autonomy and emotions. *Journal of Vocational Behavior, 59*(3), 291–309.

Fraser, N. (2009). *Scales of justice: Reimagining political space in a globalizing world.* New York, NY: Columbia University Press.

Fu, W., & Deshpande, S. P. (2014). The impact of caring climate, job satisfaction, and organizational commitment on job performance of employees in a China's insurance company. *Journal of Business Ethics, 124*(2), 339–349.

Fukushima, M., Sharp, S. F., & Kobayashi, E. (2009). Bond to society, collectivism, and conformity: A comparative study of Japanese and American college students. *Deviant Behavior, 30*(5), 434–466.

Gamoran, A., Secada, W. G., & Marrett, C. B. (2000). The organisational context of teaching and learning: Changing theoretical perspectives. In M. T. Hallinan (Ed.), *Handbook of research in the sociology of education* (pp. 37–63). New York, NY: Kluwer Academic.

Gardner W. L., Avolio B. J., Luthans F., May, D. R., & Walumbwa, F. (2005). Can you see the real me? A self-based model of authentic leaders and follower development. *Leadership Quarterly, 19*, 343–372.

Gelens, J., Dries, N., Hofmans, J., & Pepermans, R. (2013). The role of perceived organizational justice in shaping the outcomes of talent management: A research agenda. *Human Resource Management Review, 23*(4), 341–353.

Gilligan, C. (1982). *In a different voice.* Cambridge, MA: Harvard University Press.

Gilligan, C., & Attanucci, J. (1988). Two moral orientations: Gender differences and similarities. *Merrill-Palmer Quarterly, 82*, 223–237.

Global Education Monitoring Report. (2016). *Education for people and planet.* Paris, France: UNESCO Publishing.

Goffee, R., & Jones, G. (2005). Managing authenticity: The paradox of great leadership. Harvard Business Review, Retrieved from: https://hbr.org/2005/12/managing-authenticity-the-paradox-of-great-leadership

Goldhaber, D., & Cowan, J. (2014). Excavating the teacher pipeline teacher preparation programs and teacher attrition. *Journal of Teacher Education, 65*(5), 449–462.

González, N., Moll, L. C., & Amanti, C. (Eds.). (2006). *Funds of knowledge: Theorizing practices in households, communities, and classrooms.* New York, NY: Routledge.

Greenberg, J. (1990). Organizational justice: Yesterday, today, and tomorrow. *Journal of Management, 16*(2), 399–432.

Greenberg, J., & Cohen, R. L. (Eds.). (2014). *Equity and justice in social behavior.* New York, NY: Academic Press.

Greenberg, J., & Colquitt, J. A. (Eds.). (2005). *Handbook of organizational justice.* Mahwah, NJ: Lawrence Erlbaum Associates.

Greenberg, J., & Colquitt, J. A. (Eds.). (2013). *Handbook of organizational justice.* London: Psychology Press.

Greenfield, W. D. (2004). Moral leadership in schools. *Journal of Educational Administration, 42*(2), 174–196.

Greenlee, B., & Brown Jr, J. J. (2009). Retaining teachers in challenging schools. *Education, 130*(1), 96–109.

Griffin, M. L. (2003). Using critical incidents to promote and assess reflective thinking in preservice teachers. *Reflective Practice, 4*(2), 207–220.

Gross, S. J., & Shapiro, J. P. (2015). *Democratic ethical educational leadership: Reclaiming school reform.* New York, NY: Routledge.

Hackett, R. D., & Bycio, P. (1996). An evaluation of employee absenteeism as a coping mechanism among hospital nurses. *Journal of Occupational and Organizational Psychology, 69*(4), 327–338.

Hallinger, P., & Bridges, E. M. (2017). A systematic review of research on the use of problem-based learning in the preparation and development of school leaders. *Educational Administration Quarterly, 53*(2), 255–288.

Hallinger, P., & Heck, R. H. (2011). Collaborative leadership and school improvement: Understanding the impact on school capacity and student learning. *School Leadership and Management, 30*, 95–110. doi:10.1080/13632431003663214

Hansen, M., Backes, B., & Brady, V. (2016). Teacher attrition and mobility during the teach for America clustering strategy in Miami-Dade county public schools. *Educational Evaluation and Policy Analysis, 38*(3), 495–516.

Hanushek, E. A., & Woessmann, L. (2015). *The knowledge capital of nations: Education and the economics of growth.* Boston, MA: MIT Press.

Harfitt, G. J. (2015). From attrition to retention: A narrative inquiry of why beginning teachers leave and then rejoin the profession. *Asia-Pacific Journal of Teacher Education, 43*(1), 22–35.

Harrison, D. A., & Martocchio, J. J. (1998). Time for absenteeism: A 20-year review of origins, offshoots, and outcomes. *Journal of Management, 24*(3), 305–350.

Harrison, D. A., Newman, D. A., & Roth, P. L. (2006). How important are job attitudes? Meta-analytic comparisons of integrative behavioral outcomes and time sequences. *Academy of Management Journal, 49*(2), 305–325.

Hassan, S., Wright, B. E., & Yukl, G. (2014). Does ethical leadership matter in government? Effects on organizational commitment, absenteeism, and willingness to report ethical problems. *Public Administration Review, 74*(3), 333–343.

Hassard, J., Teoh, K., & Cox, T. (2016). Organizational uncertainty and stress among teachers in Hong Kong: Work characteristics and organizational justice. *Health Promotion International, 32*(5), 860–870.

He, J., & Van De Vijver, F. J. (2015). Effects of a general response style on cross-cultural comparisons: Evidence from the teaching and learning international survey. *Public Opinion Quarterly, 79*(S1), 267–290.

Henoch, J. R., Klusmann, U., Lüdtke, O., & Trautwein, U. (2015). Who becomes a teacher? Challenging the "negative selection" hypothesis. *Learning and Instruction, 36*, 46–56.

Hill, C., & Semler, S. (2001). Simulation-enhanced learning: Case studies in leadership development. *Personnel Decisions International.* Retrieved from http//:www.personn eldecisions.com/learning/pdfs/Simulation-Enhanced% 20Learning_10.pdf

Hinojosa, A. S., Gardner, W. L., Walker, H. J., Cogliser, C., & Gullifor, D. (2017). A review of cognitive dissonance theory in management research: Opportunities for further development. *Journal of Management, 43*(1), 170–199.

Ho, J. A. (2010). Ethical perception: are differences between ethnic groups situation dependent? Business Ethics - *A European Review, 19*(2). https://doi.org/10.1111/j.1467-8608.2010.01583.x

Hobfoll, S. E. (2001). The influence of culture, community, and the nested–self in the stress process: Advancing conservation of resources theory. *Applied Psychology, 50*(3), 337–421.

House, R. J., Hanges, P. J., Javidan, M., Dorfman, P. W., & Gupta, V. (eds.). (2004). *Culture, leadership, and organizations: The GLOBE study of 62 Societies.* Thousand Oaks, CA: Sage Publications.

Husu, J., & Tirri, K. (2003). A case study approach to study one teacher's moral reflection. *Teaching and Teacher Education, 19*(3), 345–357.

Ingersoll, R. M., & May, H. (2012). The magnitude, destinations, and determinants of mathematics and science teacher turnover. *Educational Evaluation and Policy Analysis, 34*(4), 435–464.

Ingersoll, R., Merrill, L., & May, H. (2016). Do accountability policies push teachers out? *Educational Leadership, 73*(8), 44–49.

Ingersoll, R., Merrill, L., & Stuckey, D. (2014). *Seven trends: The transformation of the teaching force.* CPRE Research Report # RR-80. Philadelphia, PA: Consortium for Policy Research in Education. doi:10.12698/cpre.2014.rr80

Iverson, R. D., & Deery, S. J. (2001). Understanding the "personological" basis of employee withdrawal: The influence of affective disposition on employee tardiness, early departure, and absenteeism. *Journal of Applied Psychology, 86*(5), 856.

Ivison, D. (2010). Republican human rights? *European Journal of Political Theory, 9*(1), 31–47.

Jacob, R., Goddard, R., Kim, M., Miller, R., & Goddard, Y. (2015). Exploring the causal impact of the McREL Balanced Leadership Program on leadership, principal efficacy, instructional climate, educator turnover, and student achievement. *Educational Evaluation and Policy Analysis, 37*(3), 314–332.

James, K. (2015). Culture and organizational justice: State of the literature and suggestions for future directions. In S. C. Cropanzano & L. A. Maureen (Eds.), *The Oxford handbook of justice in the workplace* (pp. 273–290). New York, NY: Oxford University Press.

Jeynes, W. H. (2015). A meta-analysis: The relationship between father involvement and student academic achievement. *Urban Education, 50*(4), 387–423.

Johns, G. (1997). Contemporary research on absence from work: Correlates, causes and consequences. *International Review of Industrial and Organizational Psychology, 12,* 115–174.

Johns, G., & Al Hajj, R. (2015). Frequency versus time lost measures of absenteeism: Is the voluntariness distinction an urban legend? *Journal of Organizational Behavior, 37*(3), 456–479.

Johnson, K. A. (2003). "Every experience is a moving force": Identity and growth through mentoring. *Teaching and Teacher Education, 19*(8), 787–800.

Joseph, P. B. (2016). Ethical reflections on becoming teachers. *Journal of Moral Education, 45*(1), 31–45.

Joy, M. M. (2016). A study on the impact of high performance work systems on employee withdrawal behaviors in information technology industry. *EPRA International Journal of Economic and Business Review, 4*(7), 213–218.

Ju, C., Lan, J., Li, Y., Feng, W., & You, X. (2015). The mediating role of workplace social support on the relationship between trait emotional intelligence and teacher burnout. *Teaching and Teacher Education, 51,* 58–67.

Kaimal, G., & Jordan, W. J. (2016). Do incentive-based programs improve teacher quality and student achievement? An analysis of implementation in 12 urban charter schools. *Teachers College Record, 118*(7), 224–240.

Kanten, P., & Ülker, F. E. (2013). The effect of organizational climate on counterproductive behaviors: An empirical study on the employees of manufacturing enterprises. *The Macrotheme Review, 2*(4), 144–160.

Kanungo, R. N. (2001). Ethical values of transactional and transformational leaders. *Canadian Journal of Administrative Sciences, 18*(4), 257–265.

Kaplan, S., Bradley, J. C., Luchman, J. N., & Haynes, D. (2009). On the role of positive and negative affectivity in job performance: A meta-analytic investigation. *Journal of Applied Psychology, 94*(1), 162–176.

Kaptein, M. (2004). Business codes of multinational firms: What do they say? *Journal of Business Ethics, 50*(1), 13–31.

Kaptein, M. (2008a). Developing and testing a measure for the ethical culture of organizations: The corporate ethical virtues model. *Journal of Organizational Behavior, 29*(7), 923–947.

Kaptein, M. (2008b). Developing a measure of unethical behavior in the workplace: A stakeholder perspective. *Journal of Management, 34*(5), 978–1008.

Kaptein, M. (2010). The ethics of organisations: A longitudinal study of the US working population. *Journal of Business Ethics, 92*(4), 601–618.

Kaptein, M. (2011). From inaction to external whistle blowing: The influence of the ethical culture of organizations on employee responses to observed wrongdoing. *Journal of Business Ethics, 98*(3), 513–530.

Keatinge, D. (2002). Versatility and flexibility: Attributes of the critical incident technique in nursing research. *Nursing & Health Sciences, 4*(1), 33–39.

Kauffman, D., S. Moore Johnson, Kardos, S.M., & Peske, H.G. (2002). "'Lost at sea': New teachers' experiences with curriculum and assessment." *Teachers College Record, 104,* 2

Kehoe, R. R., & Wright, P. M. (2013). The impact of high-performance human resource practices on employees' attitudes and behaviors. *Journal of Management, 39*(2), 366–391.

Kemppainen, J. K. (2000). The critical incident technique and nursing care quality research. *Journal of Advanced Nursing, 32*(5), 1264–1271.

Kenworthy, J., & Wong, A. (2005). Developing managerial effectiveness: Assessing and comparing the impact of development programmes using a management simulation or a management game. *Developments in Business Simulation and Experiential Learning, 32,* 164–175.

Khan, I., Nawaz, A., Qureshi, Q. A., & Khan, Z. A. (2016). The impacts of burnout, absenteeism, and commitment on intention to leave. *Journal of Education and Practice, 7*(1), 5–9.

Kish-Gephart, J. J., Harrison, D. A., & Treviño, L. K. (2010). Bad apples, bad cases, and bad barrels: Meta-analytic evidence about sources of unethical decisions at work. *Journal of Applied Psychology, 15*(1), 1–31.

Klassen, R. M., Usher, E. L., & Bong, M. (2010). Teachers' collective efficacy, Job satisfaction, and job stress in cross-cultural context. *Journal of Experimental Education, 78*(4), 464–486. DOI: 10.1080/00220970903292975

Koellner, K., & Jacobs, J. (2015). Distinguishing models of professional development: The case of an adaptive model's impact on teachers' knowledge, instruction, and student achievement. *Journal of Teacher Education, 66*(1), 51–67.

Kohlberg, L. (1986). A current statement on some theoretical issues. In S. Modgil & J. Modgil (Eds.), *Lawrence Kohlberg: Consensus and controversy* (pp. 485–546). Philadelphia, PA: Falmer Press.

Kohls, J. & Christensen, S .L. (2002). *Journal of Business Ethics, 35*: 223. https://doi.org/10.1023/A:1013822008311

Koslowsky, M. (2000). A new perspective on employee lateness. *Applied Psychology, 49*(3), 390–407.

Koslowsky, M. (2009). A multi-level model of withdrawal: Integrating and synthesizing theory and findings. *Human Resource Management Review, 19*(4), 283–303.

Koslowsky, M., Sagie, A., Krausz, M., & Singer, A. D. (1997). Correlates of employee lateness: Some theoretical considerations. *Journal of Applied Psychology, 82*(1), 79–88.

Le Mare, L., & Sohbat, E. (2002). Canadian students' perceptions of teacher characteristics that support or inhibit help seeking. *The Elementary School Journal, 102*(3), 239–253.

Lee, K., & Allen, N. J. (2002). Organizational citizenship behavior and workplace deviance: The role of affect and cognitions. *Journal of Applied Psychology, 87*(1), 131–142.

Leigh, J. P., & Lust, J. (1988). Determinants of emplyee tardiness. *Work and Occupations, 15*(1), 78–95.

Leithwood, K., & Jantzi, D. (2005). A review of transformational school leadership research 1996–2005. *Leadership and Policy in Schools, 4*(3), 177–199.

Leroy, H., Palanski, M. E., & Simons, T. (2012). Authentic leadership and behavioral integrity as drivers of follower commitment and performance. *Journal of Business Ethics, 107*(3), 255–264.

Li, S. F., & Persons, O. S. (2010) Cultural effects on business students' ethical decisions: A Chinese versus American comparison, *Journal of Education for Business, 86*(1): 10–16, DOI: 10.1080/08832321003663330

Lindqvist, P., Nordänger, U. K., & Carlsson, R. (2014). Teacher attrition the first five years – A multifaceted image. *Teaching and Teacher Education, 40*, 94–103.

Linstead, S., Maréchal, G., & Griffin, R. W. (2014). Theorizing and researching the dark side of organization. *Organization Studies, 35*(2), 165–188.

Litchka, P. R., & Shapira-Lishchinsky, O. (2016). Planning educational policy: Teacher perceptions of school principal transformational leadership in Israel and the US. *Educational Planning, 23*(2), 45–58.

Little, D. (1995) Learning as dialogue: The dependence of learner autonomy on teacher autonomy. *System 23* (2), 175–181.

Loeb, S., Miller, L. C., & Wyckoff, J. (2015). Performance screens for school improvement: The case of teacher tenure reform in New York City. *Educational Researcher, 44*(4), 199–212.

Loerbroks, A., Meng, H., Chen, M. L., Herr, R., Angerer, P., & Li, J. (2014). Primary school teachers in China: Associations of organizational justice and effort-reward imbalance with burnout and intentions to leave the profession in a cross-sectional sample. *International Archives of Occupational and Environmental Health, 87*(7), 695–703.

Long, J. S., McKenzie-Robblee, S., Schaefer, L., Steeves, P., Wnuk, S., Pinnegar, E., & Clandinin, D. J. (2012). Literature review on induction and mentoring related to early career teacher attrition and retention. *Mentoring & Tutoring: Partnership in Learning, 20*(1), 7–26.

Louws, M. L., Meirink, J. A., van Veen, K., & van Driel, J. H. (2018). Understanding teachers' professional learning goals from their current professional concerns. *Teachers and Teaching, 24*(1), 63–80.

Lucas, T., Kamble, S. V., Wu, M. S., Zhdanova, L., & Wendorf, C. A. (2016). Distributive and procedural justice for self and others: Measurement invariance and links to life satisfaction in four cultures. *Journal of Cross-Cultural Psychology, 47*(2), 234–248.

Lyons, R., Lazzara, E. H., Benishek, L. E., Zajac, S., Gregory, M., Sonesh, S. C., & Salas, E. (2015). Enhancing the effectiveness of team debriefings in medical simulation: More best practices. *Joint Commission Journal on Quality and Patient Safety, 41*(3), 115–125.

Malaklolunthu, S., & Shamsudin, F. (2011). Challenges in school-based management: Case of a "cluster school" in Malaysia. *Procedia-Social and Behavioral Sciences, 15*, 1488–1492.

Marion, R., & Gonzales, L. D. (2013). *Leadership in education: Organizational theory for the practitioner.* Long Grove, IL: Waveland Press.

Martocchio, J. J., & Jimeno, D. I. (2003). Employee absenteeism as an affective event. *Human Resource Management Review, 13*(2), 227–241.

Mathieu, J. E., Kukenberger, M. R., D'innocenzo, L., & Reilly, G. (2015). Modeling reciprocal team cohesion–performance relationships as impacted by shared leadership and members' competence. *Journal of Applied Psychology, 100*(3), 713–734.

Mausethagen, S., & Granlund, L. (2012). Contested discourses of teacher professionalism: Current tensions between education policy and teachers' union. *Journal of Education Policy, 27*(6), 815–833.

Maxwell, B., & Schwimmer, M. (2016). Seeking the elusive ethical base of teacher professionalism in Canadian codes of ethics. *Teaching and Teacher Education, 59*, 468–480.

Mayer, D. (2014). Forty years of teacher education in Australia: 1974–2014. *Journal of Education for Teaching, 40*(5), 461–473.

McGaghie, W. C., Issenberg, S. B., Petrusa, E. R., & Scalese, R. J. (2016). Revisiting "A critical review of simulation-based medical education research: 2003–2009." *Medical Education, 50*(10), 986–991.

McGrath, I. (2000). Teacher autonomy. In B. Sinclair, I. McGrath, & T. Lamb (Eds.), *Learner autonomy, teacher autonomy: Future directions* (pp. 100–110). London: Longman.

McHugh, K. A., Yammarino, F. J., Dionne, S. D., Serban, A., Sayama, H., & Chatterjee, S. (2016). Collective decision-making, leadership, and collective intelligence: Tests with agent-based simulations and a field study. *The Leadership Quarterly, 27*(2), 218–241.

McInerney, D. M., Ganotice Jr, F. A., King, R. B., Marsh, H. W., & Morin, A. J. (2015). Exploring commitment and turnover intentions among teachers: What we can learn from Hong Kong teachers. *Teaching and Teacher Education, 52*, 11–23.

Melé, D., & Sánchez-Runde, C. (2013). Cultural diversity and universal ethics in a global world. *Journal of Business Ethics, 116*(4), 681–687.

Melon, L (2018). Authentic leadership as a mediator between professional identity, organizational ethical climate and organizational citizenship behavior, organizational politics behavior and turnover among elementary school principals in Israel. Paper presented at the Israeli Society for Educational Administration & Leadership, Jerusalem, Israel.

Meyer, J. P., & Espinoza, J. A. (2016). Occupational commitment. In J. P. Meyer (Ed.), *Handbook of employee commitment* (pp. 135–145). Northhampton, MA: Edward Elgar Publishing.

Meyer, J. P., Morin, A. J., & Vandenberghe, C. (2015). Dual commitment to organization and supervisor: A person-centered approach. *Journal of Vocational Behavior, 88*, 56–72.

Meyer, J. P., Stanley, D. J., Jackson, T. A., McInnis, K. J., Maltin, E. R., & Sheppard, L. (2012). Affective, normative, and continuance commitment levels across cultures: A meta-analysis. *Journal of Vocational Behavior, 80*(2), 225–245.

Miles, D. E., Borman, W. E., Spector, P. E., & Fox, S. (2002). Building an integrative model of extra role work behaviors: A comparison of counterproductive work behavior with organizational citizenship behavior. *International Journal of Selection and Assessment, 10*(1–2), 51–57.

Miller, R. T., Murnane, R. J., & Willett, J. B. (2008). Do teacher absences impact student achievement? Longitudinal evidence from one urban school district. *Educational Evaluation and Policy Analysis, 30*(2), 181–200.

Mills, R. (2006). The Keirsey temperament model: A model for helping educational administrators facilitate ethical decision-making. *Education, 126*(3), 512–517.

Milner, H. R., & Tenore, F. B. (2010). Classroom management in diverse classrooms. *Urban Education, 45*, 560–603.

Minke, K. M., Sheridan, S. M., Kim, E. M., Ryoo, J. H., & Koziol, N. A. (2014). Congruence in parent–teacher relationships: The role of shared perceptions. *The Elementary School Journal, 114*(4), 527–546.

Minkov, M., & Hofstede, G. (2011). Is national culture a meaningful concept? Cultural values delineate homogeneous national clusters of in-country regions. *Cross-Cultural Research, 46*(2), 133–159.

Miraglia, M., & Johns, G. (2016). Going to work ill: A meta-analysis of the correlates of presenteeism and a dual-path model. *Journal of Occupational Health Psychology, 21*(3), 261–283.

Mitonga-Monga, J., & Cilliers, F. (2015). Ethics culture and ethics climate in relation to employee engagement in a developing country setting. *Journal of Psychology in Africa, 25*(3), 242–249.

Monteiro, A. R. (2015). *The teaching profession: Present and future.* New York, NY: Springer International Publishing.

Montes, S. D., Rousseau, D. M., & Tomprou, M. (2015). Psychological contract theory. *Wiley Encyclopedia of Management, 11*, 1–5.

Moorman, R. H. (1991). Relationship between organizational justice and organizational citizenship behaviors: Do fairness perceptions influence employee citizenship? *Journal of Applied Psychology, 76*, 845–855.

Moorman, R. H., & Byrne, Z. S. (2013). How does organizational justice affect organizational citizenship behavior? In J. Greenberg & J. Colquitt (Eds.), *Handbook of organizational justice* (pp. 355–380). Mahwah, NJ: Lawrence Erlbaum.

Moratis, L., Hoff, J., & Reul, B. (2006). A dual challenge facing management education: Simulation-based learning and learning about CSR. *Journal of Management Development, 25*(3), 213–231.

Morin, A. J., Meyer, J. P., McInerney, D. M., Marsh, H. W., & Ganotice Jr, F. A. (2015). Profiles of dual commitment to the occupation and organization: Relations to well-being and turnover intentions. *Asia Pacific Journal of Management, 32*(3), 717–744.

Mowday, R. T., Porter, L. W., & Steers, R. M. (2013). *Employee–organization linkages: The psychology of commitment, absenteeism, and turnover.* New York, NY: Academic Press.

Mullis, I. V. S., Martin, M. O., Foy, P., & Hooper, M. (2016). *TIMSS 2015 international results in mathematics.* Boston, MA: TIMSS & PIRLS International Study Center at Boston College.

Mullis, I. V. S., Martin, M. O., & Loveles, T. (2016). *20 Years of TIMSS: International trends in mathematics and science achievement, curriculum, and instruction.* Boston, MA: TIMSS & PIRLS International Study Center, Lynch School of Education, Boston College.

Muthén, L. K., & Muthén, B. O. (2017). *Mplus user's guide* (8th ed.). Los Angeles, CA: Muthén & Muthén.

National Policy Board for Educational Administration. (2002). Standards for principals, superintendents, curriculum directors, and supervisors. Retrieved from: http://www.npbea.org,

Nätti, J., Oinas, T., Härmä, M., Anttila, T, & Kandolin, I. (2014). Combined effects of shift-work and individual working time control on long-term sickness absence: A prospective study of Finnish employees. *Journal of Occupational and Environmental Medicine, 56*(7), 732–738.

Neal, M. B., Chapman, N. J., Ingersoll-Dayton, B., & Emlen, A. C. (1994). *Balancing work and caregiving for children, adults, and elders.* Newbury Park, CA: SAGE.

Nicholson, N., & Goodge, P. M. (1976). The influence of social, organizational, and biographical factors on female absence. *Journal of Management Studies, 13*(3), 234–254.

Niemi, H., Toom, A., & Kallioniemi, A. (Eds.). (2016). *Miracle of education: The principles and practices of teaching and learning in Finnish schools.* Rotterdam, The Netherlands: Sense Publishers.

Nilsson, P. (2009). From lesson plan to new comprehension: Exploring student teachers' pedagogical reasoning in learning about teaching. *European Journal of Teacher Education, 32*(3), 239–258.

Ning, H. K., Lee, D., & Lee, W. O. (2015). Relationships between teacher value orientations, collegiality, and collaboration in school professional learning communities. *Social Psychology of Education, 18*(2), 337–354.

Norberg, K., & Johansson, O. (2007). Ethical dilemmas of Swedish school leaders: Contrasts and common themes. *Educational Management Administration & Leadership, 35*(2), 277–294.

Normore, A. H. (2011). Ethical decision-making in school administration: Leadership as moral architecture. *Journal of Educational Administration, 49*(1), 95–97.

Normore, A. H., & Brooks, J. S. (Eds.). (2014). *Educational leadership for ethics and social justice: Views from the social sciences.* Charlotte, NC: Information Age Publishing.

North, C. (2008). What is all this talk about "social justice"? Mapping the terrain of education's latest catchphrase. *The Teachers College Record, 110*(6), 1182–1206.

O'Neill, J., & Bourke, R. (2010). Educating teachers about a code of ethical conduct. *Ethics and Education, 5*(2), 159–172.

Oplatka, I. (2009). The field of educational administration: A historical overview of scholarly attempts to recognize epistemological identities, meanings and boundaries from the 1960s onwards. *Journal of Educational Administration, 47*(1), 8–35.

Oplatka, I., & Addi-Raccah, A. (2009). Is "educational leadership" a national-contextual field of study? Some insights from an analysis of the field's major journals. In A. W. Wiseman (Ed.), *Educational leadership: Global contexts and international comparisons* (*International perspectives on education and society,* Vol. 11, pp. 399–418). London: Emerald Group Publishing.

Organ, D. W. (1988). *Organizational citizenship behavior: The good soldier syndrome.* Lexington, MA: Lexington Books.

Organ, D. W. (1997). Organizational citizenship behavior: It's construct clean-up time. *Human Performance, 10*(2), 85–97.

Organ, D. W., & Ryan, K. (1995). A meta-analytic review of attitudinal and dispositional predictors of organizational citizenship behavior. *Personnel Psychology, 48*(4), 775–802.

Orme, G., & Ashton, C. (2003). Ethics: A foundation competency. *Industrial and Commercial Training, 35*(5), 184–190.

Orphanos, S., & Orr, M. T. (2014). Learning leadership matters: The influence of innovative school leadership preparation on teachers' experiences and outcomes. *Educational Management Administration & Leadership, 42*(5), 680–700.

Page, T. M. (2015). Common pressures, same results? Recent reforms in professional standards and competences in teacher education for secondary teachers in England, France and Germany. *Journal of Education for Teaching, 41*(2), 180–202.

Pate, J., & Scullion, H. (2016). The flexpatriate psychological contract: A literature review and future research agenda. *The International Journal of Human Resource Management.* doi:10.1080/09585192.2016.1244098

Piccoli, B., & De Witte, H. (2015). Job insecurity and emotional exhaustion: Testing psychological contract breach versus distributive injustice as indicators of lack of reciprocity. *Work & Stress, 29*(3), 246–263.

Pillai, R., Williams, E. S., & Justin Tan, J. (2001). Are the scales tipped in favor of procedural or distributive justice? An investigation of the US, India, Germany, and Hong Kong (China). *International Journal of Conflict Management, 12*(4), 312–332.

Poisson, M. (2009). *Guidelines for the design and effective use of teacher codes of conduct.* Paris, France: International Institute for Educational Planning, UNESCO.

Powell, K. C., & Kalina, C. J. (2009). Cognitive and social constructivism: Developing tools for an effective classroom. *Education, 130*(2), 241–251.

Priestley, M., Miller, K., Barrett, L., & Wallace, C. (2011). Teacher learning communities and educational change in Scotland: The Highland experience. *British Educational Research Journal, 37*(2), 265–284.

Rausch, A., Lindquist, T., & Steckel, M. (2014). A test of US versus Germanic European ethical decision-making and perceptions of moral intensity: Could ethics differ within Western culture? *Journal of Managerial Issues, 26*(3), 259–283.

Regulation of the teachers' council of Thailand on professional standards and ethics. (2005). Retrieved from: http://teachercodes.iiep.unesco.org/teachercodes/codes/Asia/Thailand.pdf

Resh, N., & Sabbagh, C. (2014). Sense of justice in school and civic attitudes. *Social Psychology of Education, 17*(1), 51–72.

Richardson, V., & Fenstermacher, G. D. (2001). Manner in teaching: The study in four parts. *Journal of Curriculum Studies, 33*(6), 631–637.

Richardson, P. W., & Watt, H. M. G. (2016). Factors influencing teaching choice: Why do future teachers choose the career? In J. Loughran & M. L. Hamilton (Eds.), *International handbook of teacher education* (pp. 275–304). Singapore: Springer. doi:10.1007/978-981-10-0369-1_8

Riivari, E., & Lämsä, A. M. (2014). Does it pay to be ethical? Examining the relationship between organisations' ethical culture and innovativeness. *Journal of Business Ethics, 124*(1), 1–17.

Risku, M., Bjork, L. G., & Browne-Ferrigno, T. (2012). School–parent relations in Finland. *Journal of School Public Relations, 3*(1), 48–71.

Roach, V., Smith, L. W., & Boutin, J. (2011). School leadership policy trends and developments: Policy expediency or policy excellence? *Educational Administration Quarterly, 47*(1), 71–113.

Robinson, S. L., & Morrison, E. W. (2000). The development of psychological contract breach and violation: A longitudinal study. *Journal of Organizational Behavior, 21*, 525–546.

Rodwell, J., & Gulyas, A. (2013). The impact of the psychological contract, justice and individual differences: Nurses take it personally when employers break promises. *Journal of Advanced Nursing, 69*(12), 2774–2785.

Romme, A. G. L. (2004). Unanimity rule and organizational decision-making: A simulation model. *Organization Science, 15*(6), 704–718.

Ronfeldt, M., Farmer, S. O., McQueen, K., & Grissom, J. A. (2015). Teacher collaboration in instructional teams and student achievement. *American Educational Research Journal, 52*(3), 475–514.

Ronfeldt, M., Loeb, S., & Wyckoff, J. (2013). How teacher turnover harms student achievement. *American Educational Research Journal, 50*(1), 4–36.

Rosenal, L. (1995). Exploring the learner's world: Critical incident methodology. *The Journal of Continuing Education in Nursing, 26*(3), 115–118.

Rosenblatt, Z., & Peled, D. (2002). School ethical climate and parental involvement. *Journal of Educational Administration, 40*(4), 349–367.

Rosenblatt, Z., & Shapira-Lishchinsky, O. (2017). Temporal withdrawal behaviors in an educational policy context. *International Journal of Educational Management, 31*(7), 895–907.

Rosenblatt, Z., Shapira-Lishchinsky, O., & Shirom, A. (2010). Absenteeism in Israeli school teachers: An organizational ethics perspective. *Human Resource Management Review, 20*, 247–259.

Rosenblatt, Z., & Shirom, A. (2005). Predicting teacher absenteeism by personal background factors. *Journal of Educational Administration, 43*(2), 209–225.

Rosenblatt, Z., & Shirom, A. (2006). School ethnicity and governance influences on work absence of teachers and school administrators. *Educational Administration Quarterly, 42*(3), 361–384.

Roth, P. L., Purvis, K. L., & Bobko, P. (2012). A meta-analysis of gender group differences for measures of job performance in field studies. *Journal of Management, 38*(2), 719–739.

Ruiz-Palomino, P., & Martínez-Cañas, R. (2014). Ethical culture, ethical intent, and organisational citizenship behavior: The moderating and mediating role of person-organisation fit. *Journal of Business Ethics, 120*(1), 95–108.

Ruiz-Palomino, P., Martínez-Cañas, R., & Fontrodona, J. (2013). Ethical culture and employee outcomes: The mediating role of person-organization fit. *Journal of Business Ethics, 116*(1), 173–188.

Rupp, D. E., Shapiro, D. L., Folger, R., Skarlicki, D. P., & Shao, R. (2017). A critical analysis of the conceptualization and measurement of organizational justice: Is it time for reassessment? *Academy of Management Annals, 11*(2), 919–959.

Sachs, J. (2016). Teacher professionalism: Why are we still talking about it? *Teachers and Teaching, 22*(4), 413–425.

Sackett, P. R. (2002). The structure of counterproductive work behaviors: Dimensionality and relationships with facets of job performance. *International Journal of Selection and Assessment, 10*, 5–11.

Sackett, P. R., Berry, C. M., Wiemann, S. A., & Laczo, R. M. (2006). Citizenship and counterproductive behavior: Clarifying relations between the two domains. *Human Performance, 19*, 441–464.

Sagie, A., Birati, A., & Tziner, A. (2002). Assessing the costs of behavioral and psychological withdrawal: A new model and an empirical illustration. *Applied Psychology, 51*(1), 67–89.

Sagie, A., Elizur, D., & Koslowsky, M. (1996). Work values: A theoretical overview and a model of their effects. *Journal of Organizational Behavior, 17*(S1), 503–514.

Sagie, A. (1998). Employee absenteeism, organizational commitment, and job satisfaction: Another look. *Journal of Vocational Behavior, 52*(2), 156–171.

Salas, E., Wildman, J. L., & Piccolo, R. F. (2009). Using simulation-based training to enhance management education. *Academy of Management Learning & Education, 8*(4), 559–573.

Sami, A., Jusoh, A., Mahfar, M., Qureshi, M. I., & Khan, M. M. (2016). Role of ethical culture in creating public value. *International Review of Management and Marketing, 6*(4), 255–261.

Samuelsson, K., & Lindblad, S. (2015). School management, cultures of teaching and student outcomes: Comparing the cases of Finland and Sweden. *Teaching and Teacher Education, 49*, 168–177.

Santisi, G., Magnano, P., Hichy, Z., & Ramaci, T. (2014). Metacognitive strategies and work motivation in teachers: An empirical study. *Procedia-Social and Behavioral Sciences, 116*, 1227–1231.

Savoldelli, G. L., Naik, V. N., Hamstra, S. J., & Morgan, P. J. (2005). Barriers to use of simulation-based education. *Canadian Journal of Anesthesia, 52*(9), 944–950.

Schein, E. H. (2010). *Organizational culture and leadership.* San Francisco, CA: John Wiley & Sons.

Scheurich, J. J., & Skrla, L. (2003). *Leadership for equity and excellence: Creating high-achievement classrooms, schools, and districts.* Thousand Oaks, CA: Corwin Press.

Schleicher, A. (2015). Schools for 21st-century learners: Strong leaders, confident teachers, innovative approaches. In *International summit on the teaching profession*. Paris, France: OECD Publishing.

Schneider, B., González-Romá, V., Ostroff, C., & West, M. A. (2017). Organizational climate and culture: Reflections on the history of the constructs in the Journal of Applied Psychology. *Journal of Applied Psychology, 102*(3), 468.

Schweisfurth, M. (2013). *Learner-centered education in international perspective. Whose pedagogy for whose development?* London: Routledge.

Scott, S., Webber, C. F., Lupart, J. L., Aitken, N., & Scott, D. E. (2014). Fair and equitable assessment practices for all students. *Assessment in Education: Principles, Policy & Practice, 21*(1), 52–70.

Senk, S. L., Tatt, M. T., Reckanse, M., Rowley, G., Peck, R., & Bankov, K. (2012). Knowledge of future primary teachers for teaching mathematics: An international comparative study. *The International Journal of Mathematics Education, 44*(3), 307–324.

Sergiovanni, T. (1996). *Leadership for the schoolhouse*. San Francisco, CA: Jossey-Bass.

Shantz, A., & Alfes, K. (2015). Work engagement and voluntary absence: The moderating role of job resources. *European Journal of Work and Organizational Psychology, 24*(4), 530–543.

Shapira-Lishchinsky, O. (2007). Israeli teachers' perceptions of lateness: A gender comparison. *Sex Roles, 57*(3/4), 187–199.

Shapira-Lishchinsky, O. (2009a). Israeli male versus female teachers' intent to leave work. *Gender in Management – An International Journal, 24*(7), 543–559.

Shapira-Lishchinsky, O. (2009b). Towards professionalism: Ethical perspectives of Israeli teachers. *European Journal of Teacher Education, 32*(4), 473–487.

Shapira-Lishchinsky, O. (2010). Ethical dilemmas in teaching and nursing: The Israeli case. *Oxford Review of Education, 36*(6), 731–748.

Shapira-Lishchinsky, O. (2011). Teachers' critical incidents: Ethical dilemmas in teaching practice. *Teaching and Teacher Education, 27*, 648–656.

Shapira-Lishchinsky, O. (2012) Teachers' withdrawal behaviors: Integrating theory and findings. *Journal of Educational Administration, 50*(3), 307–326.

Shapira-Lishchinsky, O. (2013a). Team-based simulations: Learning ethical conduct in teacher trainee programs. *Teaching and Teacher Education, 33*, 1–12.

Shapira-Lishchinsky, O. (2013b). An ethical approach to teachers' dysfunctional behaviors: Voluntary lateness and voluntary absence. *Educational Practice and Theory, 35*(2), 63–84.

Shapira-Lishchinsky, O. (2014). Toward developing authentic leadership: Team based simulations. *Journal of School Leadership, 24*(5), 979–1013.

Shapira-Lishchinsky, O. (2015). Simulation-based constructivist approach for education leaders. *Educational Management Administration & Leadership, 43*(6), 972–988.

Shapira-Lishchinsky, O. (2016). From ethical reasoning to teacher education for social justice. *Teaching and Teacher Education, 60*, 245–255.

Shapira-Lishchinsky, O. (2018a). School ethical culture in TIMSS international assessments. Paper presented at the Oxford Education Symposium, St. Hugh's College, Oxford.

Shapira-Lishchinsky, O. (2018b). Exploring school ethical culture: A cross-national perspective. Paper presented at the 62nd Annual Meeting of the Comparative and International Education Society, Mexico City, Mexico.

Shapira-Lishchinsky, O., & Even-Zohar, S. (2011). Withdrawal behaviors syndrome: An ethical perspective. *Journal of Business Ethics, 103*(3), 429–451.

Shapira-Lishchinsky, O., & Gilat, I. Z. (2015). Official policies and "teachers' tendency to act": Exploring the discrepancies in teachers' perceptions. *Education Policy Analysis Archives, 23*(82), 1–20.

Shapira-Lishchinsky, O., & Ishan, G. (2013). Teachers' acceptance of absenteeism: Towards developing a specific scale. *Journal of Educational Administration, 51*(5), 594–617.

Shapira-Lishchinsky, O., & Levy-Gazenfrantz, T. (2015). Authentic leadership strategies in support of mentoring processes. *School Leadership & Management, 35*(2), 183–201.

Shapira-Lishchinsky, O., & Raftar-Ozery, T. (2016). School leadership, absenteeism acceptance, and school ethical climate as predictors of voluntary absence and organizational citizenship behaviors. *Educational Management Administration & Leadership, 44*, 1–20.

Shapira-Lishchinsky, O., & Rosenblatt, Z. (2009a). Perceptions of organizational ethics as predictors of work absence: A test of alternative absence measures. *Journal of Business Ethics, 88*(4), 717–734.

Shapira-Lishchinsky, O., & Rosenblatt, Z. (2009b). Organizational ethics and teachers' intent to leave: An integrative approach. *Educational Administration Quarterly, 45*(5), 725–758.

Shapira-Lishchinsky, O., & Rosenblatt, Z. (2010). School ethical climate and teachers' voluntary absence. *Journal of Educational Administration, 48*(2), 164–181.

Shapira-Lishchinsky, O., & Tsemach, S. (2014). Psychological empowerment as a mediator between teachers' perceptions of authentic leadership and their withdrawal and citizenship behaviors. *Educational Administration Quarterly, 50*(4), 675–712.

Shapiro, J. P., & Gross, S. J. (2013). *Ethical educational leadership in turbulent times: (Re) solving moral dilemmas* (2nd edition). New York, NY: Routledge.

Shapiro, J. P., & Stefkovich, J. A. (2010). *Ethical leadership and decision-making in education: Applying theoretical perspectives to complex dilemmas* (3rd ed.). New York, NY: Routledge.

Shapiro, J. P., & Stefkovich, J. A. (2016). *Ethical leadership and decision-making in education: Applying theoretical perspectives to complex dilemmas* (4th ed.). New York, NY: Routledge.

Shapiro, J. P., & Stefkovich, J. A. (2011). *Ethical leadership and decision making in education: Applying theoretical perspectives to complex dilemmas* (3rd ed.). New York, NY: Routledge.

Shields, C. M. (2010). Transformative leadership: Working for equity in diverse contexts. *Educational Administration Quarterly, 46*(4), 558–589.

Shiraev, E.,B. & Levy, D.A. (2015). *Cross-cultural psychology: Critical thinking and contemporary applications* (5th ed.). New York, NY: Routledge.

Sikes, P., Measor, L., & Woods, P. (2001). Critical phases and incidents. In J. Soler, A. Craft, & H. Burgess (Eds.), *Teacher development: Exploring our own practice* (pp. 104–115). Thousand Oaks, CA: SAGE Publishing.

Silva, P., Slater, C. L., Lopez-Gorosave, G., Cerdas, V., Torres, N., Antunez, S., & Briceno, F. (2017). Educational leadership for social justice in Costa Rica, Mexico, and Spain. *Journal of Educational Administration, 55*(3), 316–333.

Simon, N. S., & Moore Johnson, S. (2013). Teacher turnover in high-poverty schools: What we know and can do. Working Paper: Project on the Next Generation of Teachers. Cambridge, MA: Harvard Graduate School of Education.

Sims, R. L. (2002). Ethical rule breaking by employees: A test of social bonding theory. *Journal of Business Ethics, 40*(2), 101–109.

Sims, R. R., & Felton, E. L. (2006). Designing and delivering business ethics teaching and learning. *Journal of Business Ethics, 63*(3), 297–312.

Singh, J. B. (2006). Ethics programs in Canada's largest corporations Business and Society Review, 111(2), 119–136. https://doi.org/10.1111/j.1467-8594.2006.00264.x

Skrla, L., Scheurich, J. J., Garcia, J., & Nolly, G. (2004). Equity audits: A practical leadership tool for developing equitable and excellent schools. *Educational Administration Quarterly, 40*(1), 133–161.

Smith, E. (2011). Teaching critical reflection. *Teaching in Higher Education, 16*(2), 211–223.

Smith, M. (1972). Equality of educational opportunity. In F. Mosteller and D. P. Moynihan (Eds.), *On equality of educational opportunity* (pp. 230–342). New York, NY: Random House.

Smith, R., & Smith, R. K. (2016). *Textbook on international human rights.* Oxford: Oxford University Press.

Somech, A., & Drach-Zahavy, A. (2000). Understanding extra-role behavior in schools: The relationships between job satisfaction, sense of efficacy and teachers' extra-role behavior. *Teaching and Teacher Education, 16,* 649–659.

Starratt, R. J. (1991). Building an ethical school: A theory for practice in educational leadership. *Educational Administration Quarterly, 27*(2), 185–202.

Starratt, R. J. (2004). *Ethical leadership.* San Francisco, CA: Jossey-Bass.

Starratt, R. J. (2005). Ethical leadership. In D. Brent (Ed.), *The essentials of school leadership* (pp. 61–74). Thousand Oaks, CA: SAGE.

Starratt, R. J. (2007). Leading a community of learners: Learning to be moral by engaging the morality of learning. *Educational Management Administration & Leadership, 35*(2), 165–183.

Staw, B. M., & Oldham, G. R. (1978). Reconsidering our dependent variables: A critique and empirical study. *The Academy of Management Journal, 21*(4), 539–559.

Staw, B. M., & Ross, J. (1987). Behavior in escalation situations: Antecedents, prototypes, and solutions. *Research in Organizational Behavior, 9,* 39–78.

Stefkovich, J., & Begley, P. T. (2007). Ethical school leadership: Defining the best interests of students. *Educational Management Administration & Leadership, 35*(2), 205–224.

Strike, K. A., Haller, E. J., & Soltis, J. F. (2005). *The ethics of school administration.* New York, NY: Teachers College Press.

Strike, K., & Soltis, J. F. (2015). *The ethics of teaching.* New York, NY: Teachers College Press.

Stromquist, N. P., & Monkman, K. (2014). *Globalization and education: Integration and contestation across cultures.* Lanham, MD: Rowman & Littlefield Publishers.

Struyven, K., & Vanthournout, G. (2014). Teachers' exit decisions: An investigation into the reasons why newly qualified teachers fail to enter the teaching profession or why those who do enter do not continue teaching. *Teaching and Teacher Education, 43,* 37–45.

Sugand, K., Akhtar, K., Khatri, C., Cobb, J., & Gupte, C. (2015). Training effect of a virtual reality haptics-enabled dynamic hip screw simulator: A randomized controlled trial. *Acta Orthopaedica, 86*(6), 695–701.

Swanson, R. A., & Holton, E. F. (1999). *Results: How to assess performance, learning, and perceptions in organizations.* San Francisco, CA: Berrett-Koehler Publishers.

Tarigan, V., & Ariani, D. W. (2015). Empirical study relations job satisfaction, organizational commitment, and turnover intention. *Advances in Management and Applied Economics, 5*(2), 21–32.

Taylor, J. M., Gilligan, C., & Sullivan, A. M. (1997). *Between voice and silence: Women and girls, race and relationship.* Cambridge, MA: Harvard University Press.

Tellez, K. (2016). *An analysis of the structure and assessment of standards for teacher candidates and programs. Preparing teachers to implement college and career readiness standards: Integrating research, policy, and practice.* Rotterdam, The Netherlands: Sense Publishers.

Tenhiälä, A., Linna, A., von Bonsdorff, M., Pentti, J., Vahtera, J., Kivimäki, M., & Elovainio, M. (2013). Organizational justice, sickness absence, and employee age. *Journal of Managerial Psychology, 28*(7/8), 805–825.

Terry, H. (2011). *Golden rules and silver rules of humanity.* Concord, MA: Infinite Publishing.

Thavikulwat, P. (2009). Social choice in a computer-assisted simulation. *Simulation & Gaming, 40*(4), 488–512.

Thornberg, R. (2008). The lack of professional knowledge in values education. *Teaching and Teacher Education, 24*(7), 1791–1798.

Thornton, G. C., Mueller-Hanson, R. A., & Rupp, D. E. (2017). *Developing organizational simulations: A guide for practitioners, students, and researchers.* Mahwah, NJ: Taylor & Francis.

Tirri, K., & Husu, J. (2002). Care and responsibility in "the best interest of the child": Relational voices of ethical dilemmas in teaching. *Teachers and Teaching: Theory and Practice, 8*(1), 65–80.

Tirri, K., & Koro-Ljungberg, M. (2002). Critical incidents in the lives of gifted female Finnish scientists. *Journal of Secondary Gifted Education, 13*(4), 151–163.

Treviño, L. K., Butterfield, K. D., & McCabe, D. L. (1998). The ethical context in organizations: Influences on employee attitudes and behaviors. *Business Ethics Quarterly, 8*(3), 447–476.

Treviño, L. K., Weaver, G. R., & Reynolds, S. J. (2006). Behavioral ethics in organizations: A review. *Journal of Management, 32*(6), 951–990.

Treviño, L. K., & Youngblood, S. A. (1990). Bad apples in bad barrels: A causal analysis of ethical decision-making behavior. *Journal of Applied Psychology, 75*(4), 378.

Tripp, D. (2011). *Critical incidents in teaching: Developing professional judgement* (classic ed.). New York, NY: Routledge.

Tullberg, J. (2015). The golden rule of benevolence versus the silver rule of reciprocity. *Journal of Religion and Business Ethics, 3*(1), 223–354.

Van Nuland, S. (2011) Teacher education in Canada, *Journal of Education for Teaching, 3*(4), 409–421, DOI: 10.1080/02607476.2011.611222

Van Dyne, L., & LePine, J. A. (1998). Helping and voice extra-role behaviors: Evidence of construct and predictive validity. *Academy of Management Journal, 41*(1), 108–119.

Van Yperen, N. W., Berg, A. E., & Willering, M. C. (1999). Towards a better understanding of the link between participation in decision-making and organizational citizenship behaviour: A multilevel analysis. *Journal of Occupational and Organizational Psychology, 72*(3), 377–392.

Vardaman, J. M., Gondo, M. B., & Allen, D. G. (2014). Ethical climate and pro-social rule breaking in the workplace. *Human Resource Management Review, 24*(1), 108–118.

Vardi, Y. (2001). The effects of organizational and ethical climates on misconduct at work. *Journal of Business Ethics, 29*, 325–337.

Vardi, Y., & Weitz, E. (2016). *Misbehavior in organizations: A dynamic approach.* New York, NY: Routledge.

Victor, B., & Cullen, J. B. (1988). The organizational bases of ethical work climates. *Administrative Science Quarterly, 33*(1), 101–125.

Vigoda-Gadot, E., Beeri, I., Birman-Shemesh, T., & Somech, A. (2007). Group-level organizational citizenship behavior in the education system: A scale reconstruction and validation. *Educational Administration Quarterly, 43*(4), 462–493.

Wahlstrom, K. L., & Louis, K. S. (2008). How teachers experience principal leadership: The roles of professional community, trust, efficacy, and shared responsibility. *Educational Administration Quarterly, 44*(4), 458–495.

Walker, A., & Shuangye, C. (2007). Leader authenticity in intercultural school contexts. *Educational Management Administration and Leadership, 35*(2), 185–204.

Wallace, J. C., Edwards, B. D., Paul, J., Burke, M., Christian, M., & Eissa, G. (2016). Change the referent? A meta-analytic investigation of direct and referent-shift consensus models for organizational climate. *Journal of Management, 42*(4), 838–861.

Wang, C., & Bird, J. J. (2011). Multi-level modeling of principal authenticity and teachers' trust and engagement. *Academy of Educational Leadership Journal., 15*(4). Retrieved from: http://www.freepatentsonline.com/article/Academy-Educational-Leadership-Journal/263157472.html

Wang, H., Hall, N. C., & Rahimi, S. (2015). Self-efficacy and causal attributions in teachers: Effects on burnout, job satisfaction, illness, and quitting intentions. *Teaching and Teacher Education, 47*, 120–130.

Wang, Y. D., & Hsieh, H. H. (2013). Organizational ethical climate, perceived organizational support, and employee silence: A cross-level investigation. *Human Relations, 66*(6), 783–802.

Wang, J., Odell, .J. Klecka, C.L., Spalding, E., & Lin, E. (2011). Understanding teacher education reform. *Journal of Teacher Education, 6*(15), 395–402.

Weatherspoon, D. L., Phillips, K., & Wyatt, T. H. (2015). Effect of electronic interactive simulation on senior Bachelor of Science in nursing students' critical thinking and clinical judgment skills. *Clinical Simulation in Nursing, 11*(2), 126–133.

Weber, J. (1995). Influences upon organizational ethical subclimates: A multi-departmental analysis of a single firm. *Organization Science, 6*(5), 509–523.

Weiss, H. B., Lopez, M. E., & Rosenberg, H. (2010). *Beyond random acts: Family, school, and community engagement as an integral part of education reform.* National Policy Forum for Family, School, & Community Engagement. Cambridge, MA: Harvard Family Research Project.

Westheimer, J., & Kahne, J. (2004). What kind of citizen? The politics of educating for democracy. *American Educational Research Journal, 41*(2), 237–269.

White, L. T., Valk, R., & Dialmy, A. (2011). What is the meaning of "on time"? The sociocultural nature of punctuality. *Journal of Cross-Cultural Psychology, 42*(3), 482–493.

Wilder, S. (2014). Effects of parental involvement on academic achievement: A meta-synthesis. *Educational Review, 66*(3), 377–397.

Wolf, Z. R., & Zuzelo, P. R. (2006). "Never again" stories of nurses: Dilemmas in nursing practice. *Qualitative Health Research, 16*(9), 1191–1206.

Wolpin, J., & Burke, R. J. (1985). Relationships between absenteeism and turnover: A function of the measures? *Personnel Psychology, 38*(1), 57–74.

Wood, S. J., & Michaelides, G. (2016). Challenge and hindrance stressors and well-being-based work–nonwork interference: A diary study of portfolio workers. *Human Relations, 69*(1), 111–138.

Xie, J. L., & Johns, G. (2000). Interactive effects of absence culture salience and group cohesiveness: A multi-level and cross-level analysis of work absenteeism in the Chinese context. *Journal of Occupational and Organizational Psychology, 73*(1), 31–52.

Ybema, J. F., van der Meer, L., & Leijten, F. R. (2016). Longitudinal relationships between organizational justice, productivity loss, and sickness absence among older employees. *International Journal of Behavioral Medicine, 23*(5), 645–654.

Yoshino, A. (2012). The relationship between self-concept and achievement in TIMSS 2007: A comparison between American and Japanese students. *International Review of Education, 58*, 199–219.

Young, M. D., Crow, G., Orr, M. T., Ogawa, R., & Creighton, T. (2005). An educative look at "educating school leaders." *UCEA Review, 47*(2), 1–5.

Yusko, K. P., & Goldstein, H. W. (1997). Selecting and developing crisis leaders using competency-based simulations. *Journal of Contingencies and Crisis Management, 5*(4), 216–223.

Zeichner, K., & Pena-Sandoval, C. (2015). Venture philanthropy and teacher education policy in the US: The role of the new schools venture fund. *Teachers College Record, 117*(6), 1–24.

Zhao, Y. (2010). Preparing globally competent teachers: A new imperative for teacher education. *Journal of Teacher Education, 61*(5), 422–431.

Zimmerman, R. D., Swider, B. W., Woo, S. E., & Allen, D. G. (2016). Who withdraws? Psychological individual differences and employee withdrawal behaviors. *Journal of Applied Psychology, 101*(4), 498.

Index